THE

SETTLE

LINE

TWO-WAY GUIDE

Leeds-Settle-Carlisle

James Wood

GREAT ORTHERN

GREAT NORTHERN BOOKS
Midland Chambers, 1 Wells Road, Ilkley, LS29 9JB

First published as *Two Way Guide to the Settle Line* (White Frog
    Productions, 1989)
Second edition — Leading Edge Press, 1993
This edition 2001

ISBN: 0 9535035 7 7

© James Wood 2001

Layout and design: Barry C. Lane
Reproduction and printing by The Amadeus Press Ltd, Bradford

British Cataloguing in Publication Data: A catalogue record for this book is
available from the British Library

Cover photographs:
Top: Steam special at Dandry Mire, October 1983 (G. W. Parry/Colour-Rail P117).
Centre: Ribblehead viaduct, May 1982 (G. W. Parry/Colour-Rail P111); *Bottom,*
left: Sprinter unit at Ribblehead (Pete Shaw Photography); *Bottom, right:* Helwith
Bridge, June 1984 (G. W. Parry/Colour-Rail P155).

Private charter steam specials are run between Settle and Carlisle on occasions and one of the popular locomotives used in the past has been the Stanier 4-6-2 'Duchess of Hamilton' based at the National Railway Museum at York. No. 46229 is seen here climbing northward at Stainforth in February 1984.   (B.C.Lane)

Your Rail Journey from Leeds to Settle and Carlisle

Travelling the 113 miles from industrial Leeds to the border city of Carlisle takes you the length of England's most spectacular railway, the Settle and Carlisle line. Beginning in Leeds, a city heavily built-up, where the station literally stands on the River Aire, your train climbs gently along the Aire valley. The landscape gets greener but with the fields still punctuated by towns and villages. By the time you pass into the Ribble valley at Hellifield it has become notably rural. Soon you are at Settle Junction, where the Settle and Carlisle railway starts with the Long Drag, a 15-mile pull to cross through the Pennines. As the gradient steepens, mostly at 1 in 100, the countryside gets bleaker with moorland and hills instead of fields. The railway passes between the Three Peaks — Pen-y-Ghent, Ingleborough and Whernside — and over the magnificent Ribblehead viaduct. After Blea Moor the line runs fairly level for ten miles, assisted by long tunnels cutting through the hills and viaducts across valleys, all keeping the railway high above the remote countryside of Dentdale and Garsdale until the summit of the line at Ais Gill, the highest point reached by any railway in England. The journey is now a long descent of the Eden valley, steep at first and high above the river in Mallerstang Common. It gets gentler as the landscape becomes less wild, passing fields, woods and red sandstone villages till your journey finishes in Carlisle.

The Settle and Carlisle railway is given an architectural unity by the design of most of its station buildings, repeated all along the line in different types of stone and sometimes brick. Houses for employees are in characteristic style, seen at stations and elsewhere beside the track. The bridges and viaducts seem to fit naturally into the landscape. Some of the activity and much of the employment associated with the railway in earlier times have now disappeared. Few of the signal boxes remain. Most of the sidings at stations, quarries and other rural industries have been lifted and many stations are unstaffed. Yet the essential railway remains to be travelled on and enjoyed today, a monument to the endeavour of a former age and very much a working railway, with Sprinter trains easily managing the gradients where steam locomotives once struggled.

Why was the railway built?

The railway from Leeds to Settle and Carlisle took 30 years to construct. It was built up in stages during the nineteenth century, a period when lines were developed by competing railway companies, each trying to increase its share of passenger and freight traffic. It began in 1846 with the opening of the railway from Leeds to Shipley and Bradford. This line was leased by the Midland Railway Company and extended the following year from Shipley to Skipton. With its headquarters in Derby the Midland Railway had been formed in 1844 by the amalgamation of three railway companies, and expansion had taken it far beyond the Midlands. After Skipton the line was continued in 1849 by the Little North Western Railway through Hellifield to Clapham and Ingleton and the following year from Clapham to Lancaster. (This company was called Little to distinguish it from the larger London and North Western Railway). The Midland made an agreement to run trains over the Little North Western's system, later taking the company over. So by 1850 Midland passengers were able to reach Lancaster and change onto the West Coast Main Line (London and North Western Railway) for Carlisle and Scotland.

In 1861 the journey was shortened. After Clapham passengers took the branch to Ingleton, changing to continue northwards on the new London and North Western line to Low Gill and then the West Coast Main Line to Carlisle (see map on page 46). But connections at Ingleton were poor. At first passengers even had to walk between the Midland and London and North Western stations. These two companies were in competition for traffic to Scotland and agreement could not be reached for the Midland to run trains right through to Carlisle and Scotland, so the company looked for a different route.

In the south too the Midland faced problems where its services used other companies' lines. Its London trains ran over the London and North Western line into Euston but were often delayed. In 1858 the opening of a new line allowed Midland trains to run on the Great Northern Railway into King's Cross. This route was unsatisfactory too so the Midland constructed its own line to a new terminus at St. Pancras, opened in 1868. To reach Scotland it proposed a 72½-mile line from Settle through Garsdale and Appleby to Carlisle, with a branch to Hawes. This had the backing of other railway companies — the Lancashire and Yorkshire, the

North British and the Glasgow and South Western. Parliament gave approval in 1866.

Meantime the Midland's shareholders were worrying about the financial burden represented by the Settle and Carlisle project in view of the costs of recent expansion to St. Pancras and also to Manchester too. The London and North Western was alarmed that the Midland would have an independent route to Scotland. So the two companies started talking again and agreed about joint use of the West Coast Main Line to Carlisle. The Midland then applied to abandon the Settle and Carlisle scheme, but was opposed by those railway companies that had earlier offered support and by local landowners. Parliament refused the abandonment in April 1869, compelling the Midland to build it.

How was it built?

The Midland Railway started construction of the line in autumn 1869, the job being let in four contracts for the main line and one for the Hawes branch. This was the last British railway built in traditional fashion, employing thousands of men, hundreds of horses, and without any of the earth-moving equipment available soon afterwards, but it was the first major engineering operation to use dynamite instead of gunpowder. Much of the route was built in remote countryside and many of the workforce came in from outside, to be accommodated in shanty towns along the line they were building. They toiled for nearly seven years, sometimes in severe conditions and extreme weather. Some died here of diseases or accidents, as graves and memorials in local churches testify. Their labour completed the Midland Railway's own route from St. Pancras to Carlisle, creating the grandest and most scenic railway in England.

As the railway was designed for main line expresses speeding between the towns and cities of England and Scotland, it was engineered to avoid tight bends and steep gradients. There are continuing gradients of course but none greater than 1 in 100, which compares favourably with the 1 in 75 at Shap on the West Coast Main Line. In the days of steam these gradients were a challenge, particularly the Long Drag, the climb north from Settle Junction up to Blea Moor, and the shorter but equally steep climb south from Crosby Garrett up to Ais Gill. The line followed the best route from an engineering viewpoint without wandering to serve towns and villages on the way — indeed in the remoter parts there are none. But local stations were provided even if sometimes at a distance from the places whose names they bear. The railway overcomes the harsh terrain with its 22 viaducts, 14 tunnels, numerous smaller bridges and many cuttings and embankments. 16 miles of it run continuously at more than a thousand feet above sea level. Ais Gill, its summit, is at 1,169 feet — compare Shap summit on the West Coast Main Line at 916 feet.

First passengers in 1876

The Settle and Carlisle railway opened for goods traffic in August 1875 and for passengers on 1 May 1876. The Midland Railway had achieved its ambition to run expresses from St. Pancras to Carlisle and Scotland. Reaching Carlisle from the south many trains divided into portions for Glasgow and Edinburgh to run over Scottish companies' lines. Southbound they would join up there. At the opening eight trains operated each way, of which three were local stopping services. St. Pancras to Glasgow took 10¾ hours at the start, soon improved to 10½ hours. The trip between Leeds and Carlisle varied from under three hours on a train with a couple of stops to over five on one calling at all stations. The Midland could not offer journey times to Scotland as quick as its two rivals on the west coast (Euston–Crewe–Carlisle) and east coast (Kings Cross–York–Berwick) routes, however it was ahead of other companies in provision of passenger comforts. In that period there were three classes of rail travel, but in 1875 the Midland had pioneered the abolition of second class, upgrading the old third with cushioned seats instead of wooden ones and reducing first-class fares to the old second-class level. The year before it had introduced Pullman cars from the USA, offering luxury travel, and these ran from the beginning over the Settle and Carlisle line. Sleeping cars operated on night trains.

The only branch, six miles of single track to Hawes, opened to passengers on 1 October 1878. On its descent from Hawes Junction (later renamed Garsdale) to Hawes this had one tunnel and two viaducts and an average gradient of 1 in 80. From Hawes the North Eastern Railway continued the line down Wensleydale to Northallerton on the East Coast Main Line.

Peacetime Improvements, Wartime and Decline

Over the years train services and timings improved. Through trains ran from Manchester to Hellifield then north via Settle to Carlisle and Scottish destinations. Through coaches operated to serve Bristol, Stranraer, Aberdeen, Inverness and other towns. Dining cars were provided from 1893 on all daytime expresses between London and Scotland. By 1901 St. Pancras to Edinburgh was possible in 8 hours 35 minutes, with Glasgow taking 15 minutes longer and even as far back as the early years of the twentieth century the Midland advertised its line as the tourist route to Scotland.

In the first world war all railways were brought under government control. The Midland carried troops and war materials, with other services slowed or curtailed. Not long afterwards in 1923 the Midland's independent existence ceased with the grouping of most British railways into four large companies. It became part of the London Midland and Scottish Railway, as did its old rival, the London and North Western. The Settle and Carlisle route assumed a lesser importance as principal services were concentrated on the West Coast Main Line. There was a little improvement to services but the railway suffered from growing competition from the bus and motor car. The principal services between St. Pancras and Glasgow and Edinburgh were given names — the *Thames-Clyde* and the *Thames-Forth* , later renamed the *Waverley*. In 1932 the *Thames-Clyde* was accelerated to make the journey in 8 hours 50 minutes, the same as the best time of 1901.

Railways were again placed under direct government control in the second world war and the Settle and Carlisle line was heavily used by freight traffic. Nationalisation of the railways followed after the war in 1948. Initially services continued much as before, but soon there were station closures — Ormside, Cotehill and Crosby Garrett in 1952, and others followed. In 1954 the passenger service from Garsdale to Northallerton was withdrawn but the Garsdale to Hawes trains continued for another five years. The Hellifield to Blackburn services ceased in 1962.

Just as an indication of the declining services of that period, look at the 1961/62 winter timetable. The timings seem more suited to railway operating convenience than planned in passengers' interests. Someone at Carlisle for instance wanting to reach Langwathby needs a local stopping train. There is a choice of three. The first departs at 8.05am, then there is a gap till 4.37pm with the final one at 6.05pm. A passenger for Leeds has more choice. Long-distance trains, taking about 2½ hours, depart at 12.59am, 12.06pm, 12.58pm, 6.55pm and 11.56pm, or else there is the local service, with a change of train and a journey time of 4 hours or more, departing at 8.05am and 4.37pm. The closure of the whole Settle and Carlisle railway was foreshadowed in 1963 in Dr. Beeching's report *The Reshaping of British Railways*. This was rejected by the government the following year. However twelve more stations between Settle and Carlisle closed in 1970 and freight services declined. *The Waverley* (the St. Pancras to Edinburgh express) ceased to run in 1968, while the *Thames-Clyde* between St. Pancras and Glasgow had its name removed in 1975 and was withdrawn the year after. In 1977 the last service from St. Pancras to Scotland, an overnight train to Glasgow, was withdrawn. There remained on the route only a service of Nottingham–Leeds–Carlisle–Glasgow trains. Between Settle and Carlisle they stopped only at Appleby, the sole station still open. These were rerouted in 1982, a low point in the line's fortunes, the

only service left being two return trains between Leeds and Carlisle on weekdays. Passengers between Settle and Carlisle could easily believe themselves on a very long and neglected branch line with a single station, at Appleby. British Rail meanwhile claimed it had no plans to close the line.

In 1974 a ramblers' group persuaded British Rail to run a day excursion from West Yorkshire to Garsdale, a station that had closed in 1970. Its success led to the establishment the following year of DalesRail, excursion trains at weekends from West Yorkshire conveying walkers to normally closed stations north of Settle. DalesRail was successful and trains continued as far as Carlisle and came from Lancashire too, via Hellifield and north through Settle. DalesRail enabled town-dwellers to reach the country and country-dwellers to make the opposite journey for a day out in town. Some 6,000 used these trains each summer.

Threatened Closure

The long decline in regular train services, the years of neglected maintenance (repairing Ribblehead viaduct could be a a vast expense — £6 million was a figure suggested in 1981) and the suspicion that British Rail wanted to close the line anyway led to the formation of the Friends of the Settle–Carlisle Line in 1981 to campaign on its behalf. In August 1983 British Rail officially notified its intention to seek closure and in December issued the official closure notice but had to issue it twice more before being sure it was legally correct. Objections to closure were lodged from 22,265 people and one dog.

In summer 1984 British Rail increased the service between Leeds and Carlisle because of passenger demand and the following summer there were Sunday trains again. Hearings into objections to closure were held in March 1986. In July eight of the closed stations reopened to additional regular services. Although "closed" the stations had been used in recent years by DalesRail excursion trains and their full reopening posed no insuperable problems. The new services were well patronised. The report in December on the objections to closure firmly rejected British Rail's case but the final decision lay with the Minister. Passenger numbers meantime grew from 93,000, who used the minimal service in 1983, to nearly half a million in 1988, on the service of five trains each way. The Minister announced in May of that year that he was minded to consent to closure but wanted a private buyer to be found for the line and asked for new evidence from passengers because of the additional stations and services. This time objectors numbered over 32,000 and the recommendation, in December, was still firmly against closure. No private buyer had emerged and a test on Ribblehead viaduct showed that repairs would cost much less than British Rail had suggested. On 11 April 1989 the Minister announced his refusal of the closure. Relief and rejoicing ended the long years of uncertainty. The period from British Rail announcing its intention to close the line and the Minister's refusal lasted nearly as long as the line's construction in Midland Railway days over a century earlier.

Revival and Future

British Rail and other parties set to work on long-neglected maintenance as well as new projects. Ribblehead viaduct was closed in autumn 1989 for repair, including the laying of a waterproof membrane under the track to prevent water ingress into the arches and piers. Othet bridges were repaired or renewed. Some station platforms were raised, some lengthened to take four-

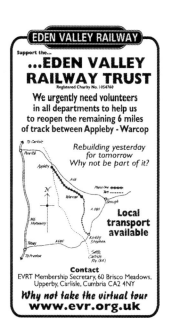

car Sprinter trains. Station buildings were repaired and lighting improved on platforms. A northbound platform was provided at Ribblehead and footbridges at Settle and Kirkby Stephen. The platform buildings at Hellifield, for years dilapidated and fenced off, were renovated in 1994. Electrification of the services from Leeds and Bradford to Ilkley and Skipton was completed in 1995. Radio signalling was introduced from Settle to Carlisle in 1993, and in 1997 Automatic Warning System was provided, to give an audible warning to the train driver of the aspect of the signal ahead. In 1991 the local authorities declared the railway from Hellifield to Carlisle a conservation area, so offering protection to the buildings and structures and opening the door to grant aid.

Between Leeds and Carlisle there are five trains each way on weekdays and more on Saturdays. A service between Leeds and Glasgow over the line started again in 1999 after an absence of 17 years. Trains run on Sundays too. Freight, long absent from the route, returned in 1994 with gypsum trains from Drax power station, near Selby, to Kirkby Thore, whose sidings were extended. The expansion in freight traffic with long heavy trains has highlighted the neglected track maintenance of past years and an extensive programme of track renewal has begun. Under rail privatisation Regional Railways North East was confirmed in 1997 as the train operating company, renamed Northern Spirit in 1998.

Full restoration of regular passenger services on the Blackburn to Hellifield line is still awaited. These will enable passengers from Manchester and north Lancashire to reach the Settle line at Hellifield and travel on to Carlisle. This is the journey made on summer Sundays by Lancashire DalesRail trains. Modernisation of signalling is needed to allow trains to run closer together and increase the line's capacity. There is still work to be done on upgrading stations and facilities to make it more attractive to use the train services. In the new century we can expect improvements on this railway, confident that it has a secure place within the country's rail network.

Some Addresses

Friends of the Settle-Carlisle Line

Founded in 1981 the Friends are a voluntary organisation who fought to save the line from closure and now support and help to develop it as a part of the national network. They campaign to improve train services and are active in practical work like painting station buildings, and maintaining the gardens. They restored the disused signal boxes at Armathwaite and Settle. At Appleby and Settle stations they have opened shops. They organise a programme of guided walks in connection with the train services. Members receive a quarterly magazine reporting on all aspects of the line. Annual membership is £8 from the Membership Secretary, 5 Dewhirst Road, Brighouse, West Yorkshire HD6 4BA. Web site — www.settle-carlisle.org

Eden Valley Railway Trust

This trust aims to reopen the North Eastern Railway from Appleby initially to Warcop (this section served an army depot till 1989) and to reinstate the line beyond. Members get a quarterly newsletter and membership costs £10 a year from the Membership Secretary, 60 Brisco Meadows, Carlisle CA2 4NY. Web site — www.evr.org.uk

Wensleydale Railway Association

The association hopes to reinstate passenger services on the 40 mile Wensleydale line from Garsdale, on the Settle and Carlisle line, to Northallerton, on the East Coast Main Line. The track is lifted on the 18 miles from Garsdale to Redmire but the track bed is mostly still there, while the 22 miles from Redmire to Northallerton are an operating railway, used by Ministry of Defence trains. Members receive a newsletter three times a year. Membership costs £9 annually from WRA Membership, PO Box 65, Northallerton, North Yorkshire DL7 8YZ. Web site — www.wensleydalerailway.com

Ribble Valley Rail

This organisation was set up to campaign for rail services on the Blackburn–Hellifield line. Between Blackburn and Clitheroe (13½ miles from Hellifield) passenger services restarted on summer Saturdays in 1990, later on all weekdays and summer Sundays. Between Clitheroe and Hellifield the only services are Lancashire DalesRail trains on summer Sundays and full reopening is still awaited. Members receive a quarterly newsletter and annual membership costs £2.50 from the Membership Secretary, 55 Bank Head Lane, Hoghton, Preston PR5 0AB.

Books and Maps

Many books have been written about this railway. For a general history look for *Settle to Carlisle* by W. R. Mitchell and David Joy, published by Dalesman Books, or *The Leeds Settle and Carlisle Railway* by Martin Bairstow, published by Martin Bairstow.

The course of the railway is shown on the following Ordnance Survey Landranger maps at 1:50,000 scale, about 1¼ inches to a mile:

Sheet   85 Carlisle & Solway Firth Gretna Green
Sheet   86 Haltwhistle & Brampton Bewcastle & Alston
Sheet   90 Penrith & Keswick Ambleside
Sheet   91 Appleby-in-Westmorland area
Sheet   98 Wensleydale & Upper Wharfedale
Sheet 103 Blackburn & Burnley Clitheroe & Skipton
Sheet 104 Leeds & Bradford Harrogate & Ilkley

Along the Line — What You Can See and Do

The Leeds–Settle–Carlisle railway journey is an experience in itself but don't forget there are lots of places worth visiting all along the line. Some are well-known, some little-known, and many are close to a station. The Waterfront and the shopping areas are near the station in **Leeds**. The station is built over the River Aire and a short walk takes you through the Dark Arches, with a turning to pass below the station you've just left. Here under vaulted roofs you cross the river and reach Granary Wharf with its many craft shops. Going outside now you reach the Leeds and Liverpool Canal, which was completed in 1816. A lock on the River Aire here is the beginning of its 127-mile course. Its towpath is ideal for anything from a short stroll to a long-distance walk. This area was the heart of nineteenth-century industrial Leeds and is now transformed into the attractive Waterfront. A riverside walk takes you to Tetley's Brewery Wharf and the Royal Armouries Museum. Many of central Leeds's shopping streets are pedestrianised. Go to the Victoria Quarter and the traditional arcades for speciality shopping. The Henry Moore sculpture collection at the City Art Gallery is of national importance. Outside central Leeds, you can visit Kirkstall Abbey, which is seen from the railway. It was founded by the Cistercian Order in 1152 and dissolved under Henry VIII in 1539. Its ruins are extensive and there is also a museum in the Abbey's gatehouse. Interesting visits can be undertaken as well to Temple Newsam House, built in Jacobean style, and the Thackray Medical Museum at St. James's Hospital.

It's worth getting off at **Saltaire** to see the model village established by Sir Titus Salt. A successful manufacturer of worsted cloth in Bradford in the middle of the nineteenth century, he moved his business away from its insanitary conditions and built mills at Saltaire with housing for employees and a church, a school, a park, an institute (community centre) and almshouses, but no pub. This building work lasted over a twenty-year period. The houses were superior to those affordable by working people at that period and each had water supply, drainage, gas, its own back yard and WC. The mill was large enough to produce 30,000 yards of cloth daily, with 3,000 employees at work there. Today in Salt's Mill you can visit the large gallery developed there, which includes works by the Bradford-born artist, David Hockney. There is a waterbus service on the canal between Shipley, Saltaire and Bingley from Easter to October. On the far side of the canal is the cable-hauled Shipley Glen Tramway, taking you to the top of the Glen. Recently restored, it operates at weekends and holiday periods.

In **Bingley** the canal is close to the railway and a short walk from the station along the towpath brings you to a three-rise set of locks, which lift the canal 30 feet. Stay with the canal a little longer and reach the famous five-rise staircase of locks lifting the canal 60 feet in less than 100 yards.

Alighting at **Keighley** you can cross to the adjacent platforms to begin a journey on the Keighley and Worth Valley Railway. Closed by British Rail in 1961, this 4¾ mile branch line was reopened by a preservation society in 1968. Its beautifully restored stations,

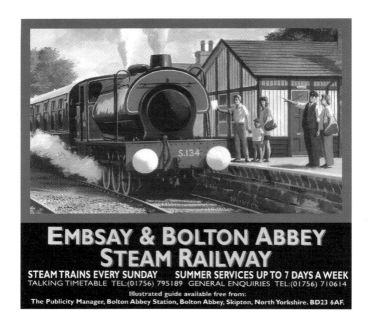

reflecting an ideal of rail travel in the 1950's, are served by steam-hauled and diesel trains. The turntable was brought to Keighley from Garsdale in 1989. The line has featured in films including *Yanks* and *The Railway Children*. One of the stations is at Haworth, the small town where the Brontë sisters lived. The steep cobbled main street with its grey stone buildings leads up to the Parsonage, which houses a museum about the Brontë family. And Britain's smallest station, Damems, is on this branch.

Skipton is a market town with a broad attractive main street approaching the parish church and the castle, which dates back to Norman times. The Clifford family held it for centuries and Lady Anne Clifford, born there in 1590, repaired it. She repaired the church too, as well as Pendragon and Appleby castles, which stand near the Settle and Carlisle railway. The Leeds and Liverpool Canal flows through Skipton. Its towpath leads you past wharves and warehouses to the short Springs Branch under the castle walls. The branch ends where limestone was once loaded from a wharf onto canal boats. Two miles from Skipton is the Embsay terminus of the Embsay & Bolton Abbey Steam Railway. From here the line that once ran to Ilkley has been reopened as far as Bolton Abbey and steam-hauled and diesel trains are operated.

Steep limestone hillsides enclose **Settle** to the east. Anyone with energy can follow footpaths up here and see Ribblesdale spread out below and Pen-y-Ghent no distance to the north. Settle has plenty of shops, pubs and cafés for the visitor and is a pleasant town to linger in, with its market place. and narrow streets of Georgian (and older) houses. The Museum of North Craven Life in Chapel Street tells you about local life and history.

At **Ribblehead** the refurbished station includes a visitor centre dealing with the railway. Nearby stands the Station Inn but there is no village here. Walking beside the railway you can admire the magnificent 24-arch viaduct. The possible costs of repairing it were for years offered as a reason for closing the line. In past times the station was a centre for the local scattered community, also a meteorological reporting point with the stationmaster sending regular readings to the Air Ministry.

Getting to **Dent** town from the station means going a whole four

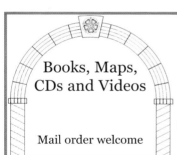

miles further down Dentdale, but with its cobbled streets and stone houses it is an attractive place. The population, larger than today in the eighteenth and nineteenth centuries, was known for hand-knitting, with whole families working to produce stockings and gloves. The poet Robert Southey described them as the terrible (meaning very fast) knitters of Dent. A granite fountain in the main street remembers Adam Sedgwick, one of the pioneers of geology, born at Dent in 1785.

Hawes, a small market town at the head of Wensleydale, is within reach of **Garsdale** station. It is the home of Wensleydale cheese, has cafés and craft workshops to visit and you can watch ropes being made at the ropeworks. The former station, once used by Garsdale to Northallerton trains on the Wensleydale line, now houses the Yorkshire Dales National Park information centre. Close by is the Dales Countryside Museum, showing you life in Wensleydale in past years.

The summit of the line is passed at **Ais Gill**, indicated on a board each side of the line. The signal box which stood here is now preserved by the Midland Railway Trust at Butterley in Derbyshire.

After Ais Gill the railway passes through **Mallerstang**, a remote area with a few isolated farms and houses and one small village, Outhgill. As Mallerstang ends and before you pass through Birkett tunnel, you catch a view of **Pendragon Castle**, which stands near the Eden. Named because of an association with Uther Pendragon, King Arthur's father, the present castle dates from the twelfth century and was last restored in 1661 by Lady Anne Clifford, who visited it frequently.

Kirkby Stephen is another place distant from its station, a mile and a half from this market town. The attractive buildings around the market square include the cloisters, which lead you to the parish church of St. Stephen, notable for its long nave, which dates back to the thirteenth century.

A plaque on **Appleby** station remembers Eric Treacy, bishop of Wakefield and railway photographer, who died here in 1978. From the station it is a short walk down into Appleby, the former county town of Westmorland. The older part of the town lies within a loop of the River Eden, with the main street, Boroughgate, leading from St. Lawrence's church up towards the castle, both dating from the twelfth century. Many of the buildings are of red sandstone quarried locally, which gives the streets a warm mellow appearance. The castle has a prominent keep and its grounds have a collection of rare birds and animals. The almshouses built in Boroughgate in the seventeenth century still serve their original purpose. Every year in early June hundreds of gypsies and other travellers gather for Appleby New Fair, some still coming in traditional caravans, meeting to buy and sell horses and race them.

A couple of miles north of **Langwathby**, where you can refresh at the Brief Encounter cafe located in the station building, is Long Meg and Her Daughters, a stone circle (in fact an oval) about four and a half thousand years old. There are some 66 stones with Long Meg, the tallest, standing outside the circle. The exact purpose is unknown but may have been to do with the rhythm of the seasons since the midwinter sun seen from the centre of the circle sets over Long Meg. Not far away are Lacy's Caves, cut out of the red sandstone above the River Eden by an eighteenth century landowner. Their purpose is also unknown, but they may have been a wine store or else a romantic folly. In Langwathby itself you can visit Eden Ostrich World to view these birds and many other animals.

Your train reaches the border city of **Carlisle** at Citadel station, a grand and spacious reminder of the great days of Britain's railways. If you've arrived hungry or thirsty, there is a wide variety of cafés and restaurants in the city and pubs as well, and the central streets with the Lanes shopping centre are well provided with shops. Carlisle is an old city; its first major settlement was built by the Romans. Hadrian's wall passed through it, marking the boundary of the empire. For many centuries Carlisle was a border stronghold, disputed between Scotland and England. The present castle was started by William II at the end of the eleventh century. It is well worth a visit to explore its passages and enjoy the views from the keep. It last saw action in 1745 when it was besieged and recaptured from Bonnie Prince Charlie's forces. The red sandstone cathedral is one of England's smallest — see especially the magnificent painted ceiling above the choir. Go to Tullie House Museum where the history of all this area over the last two thousand years is brilliantly brought to life. You will enjoy wandering Carlisle's streets. It is a compact city and all these attractions are close together, and none far from Citadel station for your return trip.

How to use this guide

The Settle Line 2 Way Guide consists of two parts. Your direction of travel — are you going towards Leeds or Carlisle? — is what determines which end of the guide you will use. Make sure you are reading the appropriate part.

The guide is written from the viewpoint of a passenger facing the direction of travel and following the journey reading up the page from bottom to top. The railway is indicated diagrammatically with every quarter mile marked like a sleeper between the rails, and every full mile shown with its number. Five miles of the route are on each page, with features of interest shown on the line to the left and right nearby.

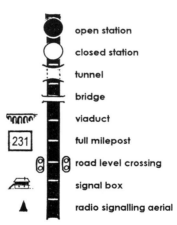

	open station
	closed station
	tunnel
	bridge
	viaduct
231	**full milepost**
	road level crossing
	signal box
	radio signalling aerial

The Midland Railway placed mileposts every quarter mile to indicate the distance to London St Pancras. Excepting about a mile outside Carlisle and Leeds, they are mostly visible, on the right going towards Carlisle or the left going towards Leeds.

Usually they are of cast iron on posts three or four feet high, beside the line or sometimes attached to buildings. The full miles have two oblong faces, angled to be seen from each direction, and the fractional distances have three faces which are also readable from both directions. Gradient posts can also be seen. They are on the opposite side of the tracks to the mileposts and are much smaller.

The Leeds & Liverpool Canal and the railway both follow the Aire valley. The train crosses the canal four times and the River Aire twelve.

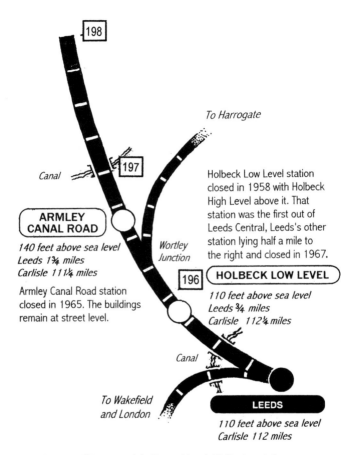

198

To Harrogate

197

Canal

ARMLEY CANAL ROAD

140 feet above sea level
Leeds 1¾ miles
Carlisle 111¼ miles

Armley Canal Road station closed in 1965. The buildings remain at street level.

Wortley Junction

Holbeck Low Level station closed in 1958 with Holbeck High Level above it. That station was the first out of Leeds Central, Leeds's other station lying half a mile to the right and closed in 1967.

196 **HOLBECK LOW LEVEL**

110 feet above sea level
Leeds ¾ miles
Carlisle 112¼ miles

Canal

To Wakefield and London

LEEDS

110 feet above sea level
Carlisle 112 miles

Trains on this route originally used Leeds Wellington station modernised in 1938 with an elegant concourse and linked to the adjacent Leeds New station to become Leeds City. This concourse, not used for passengers since 1966 has been restored for passengers again in the current regeneration work.

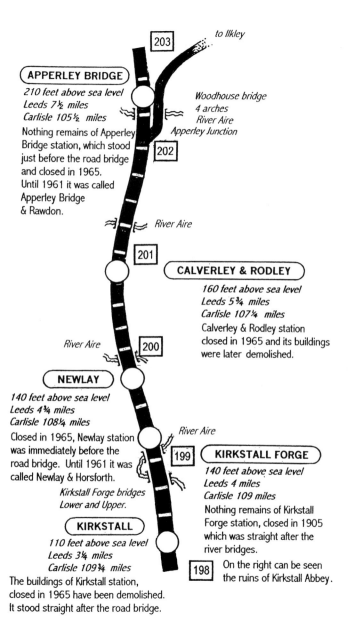

203

to Ilkley

APPERLEY BRIDGE

210 feet above sea level
Leeds 7½ miles
Carlisle 105½ miles

Nothing remains of Apperley Bridge station, which stood just before the road bridge and closed in 1965. Until 1961 it was called Apperley Bridge & Rawdon.

Woodhouse bridge
4 arches
River Aire
Apperley Junction

202

River Aire

201

CALVERLEY & RODLEY

160 feet above sea level
Leeds 5¾ miles
Carlisle 107¼ miles

Calverley & Rodley station closed in 1965 and its buildings were later demolished.

River Aire

200

NEWLAY

140 feet above sea level
Leeds 4¾ miles
Carlisle 108¼ miles

Closed in 1965, Newlay station was immediately before the road bridge. Until 1961 it was called Newlay & Horsforth.

Kirkstall Forge bridges
Lower and Upper.

River Aire

199

KIRKSTALL FORGE

140 feet above sea level
Leeds 4 miles
Carlisle 109 miles

Nothing remains of Kirkstall Forge station, closed in 1905 which was straight after the river bridges.

KIRKSTALL

110 feet above sea level
Leeds 3¼ miles
Carlisle 109¼ miles

The buildings of Kirkstall station, closed in 1965 have been demolished. It stood straight after the road bridge.

198 On the right can be seen the ruins of Kirkstall Abbey.

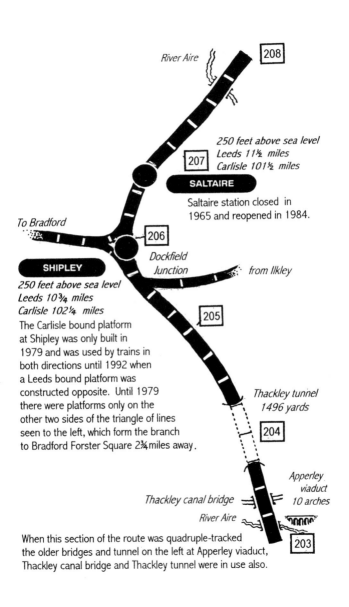

River Aire

208

250 feet above sea level
Leeds 11½ miles
Carlisle 101½ miles

207

SALTAIRE

Saltaire station closed in
1965 and reopened in 1984.

To Bradford

206

Dockfield
Junction   ∴ *from Ilkley*

SHIPLEY

250 feet above sea level
Leeds 10¾ miles
Carlisle 102¼ miles

The Carlisle bound platform
at Shipley was only built in
1979 and was used by trains in
both directions until 1992 when
a Leeds bound platform was
constructed opposite. Until 1979
there were platforms only on the
other two sides of the triangle of lines
seen to the left, which form the branch
to Bradford Forster Square 2¾ miles away.

205

Thackley tunnel
1496 yards

204

Apperley
viaduct
10 arches

Thackley canal bridge

River Aire

203

When this section of the route was quadruple-tracked
the older bridges and tunnel on the left at Apperley viaduct,
Thackley canal bridge and Thackley tunnel were in use also.

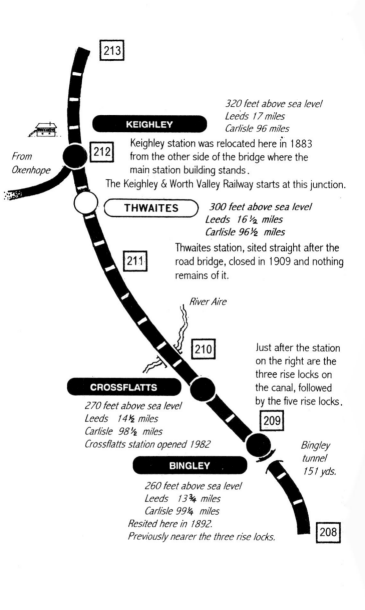

213

KEIGHLEY

320 feet above sea level
Leeds 17 miles
Carlisle 96 miles

Keighley station was relocated here in 1883 from the other side of the bridge where the main station building stands.

The Keighley & Worth Valley Railway starts at this junction.

212

From Oxenhope

THWAITES

300 feet above sea level
Leeds 16½ miles
Carlisle 96½ miles

Thwaites station, sited straight after the road bridge, closed in 1909 and nothing remains of it.

211

River Aire

210

Just after the station on the right are the three rise locks on the canal, followed by the five rise locks.

CROSSFLATTS

270 feet above sea level
Leeds 14½ miles
Carlisle 98½ miles
Crossflatts station opened 1982

209

Bingley tunnel 151 yds.

BINGLEY

260 feet above sea level
Leeds 13¾ miles
Carlisle 99¼ miles
Resited here in 1892.
Previously nearer the three rise locks.

208

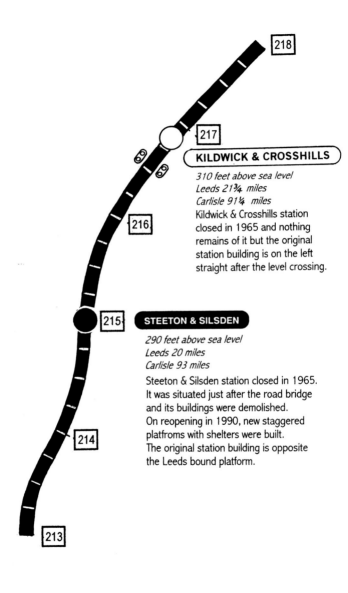

218

217

KILDWICK & CROSSHILLS

310 feet above sea level
Leeds 21¾ miles
Carlisle 91¼ miles
Kildwick & Crosshills station
closed in 1965 and nothing
remains of it but the original
station building is on the left
straight after the level crossing.

216

215

STEETON & SILSDEN

290 feet above sea level
Leeds 20 miles
Carlisle 93 miles

Steeton & Silsden station closed in 1965.
It was situated just after the road bridge
and its buildings were demolished.
On reopening in 1990, new staggered
platfroms with shelters were built.
The original station building is opposite
the Leeds bound platform.

214

213

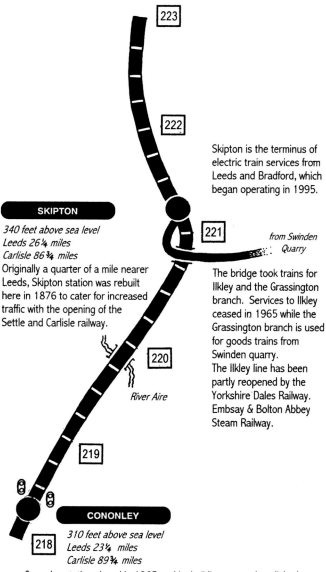

223

222

Skipton is the terminus of electric train services from Leeds and Bradford, which began operating in 1995.

SKIPTON

340 feet above sea level
Leeds 26¼ miles
Carlisle 86¾ miles
Originally a quarter of a mile nearer Leeds, Skipton station was rebuilt here in 1876 to cater for increased traffic with the opening of the Settle and Carlisle railway.

221

from Swinden Quarry

The bridge took trains for Ilkley and the Grassington branch. Services to Ilkley ceased in 1965 while the Grassington branch is used for goods trains from Swinden quarry.
The Ilkley line has been partly reopened by the Yorkshire Dales Railway. Embsay & Bolton Abbey Steam Railway.

220

River Aire

219

218

CONONLEY

310 feet above sea level
Leeds 23¼ miles
Carlisle 89¾ miles

Cononley station closed in 1965 and its buildings were demolished. On reopening in 1988, shelters were provided on both platforms.

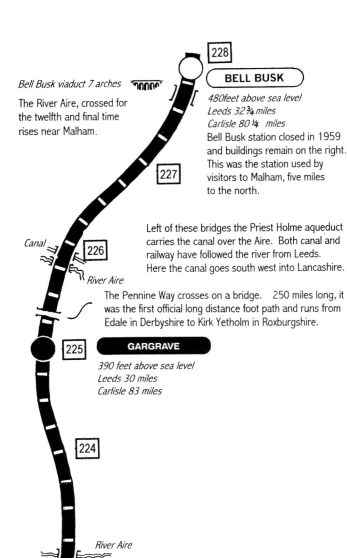

228

(**BELL BUSK**)

Bell Busk viaduct 7 arches

The River Aire, crossed for the twelfth and final time rises near Malham.

480feet above sea level
Leeds 32¾ miles
Carlisle 80¼ miles

Bell Busk station closed in 1959 and buildings remain on the right. This was the station used by visitors to Malham, five miles to the north.

227

Left of these bridges the Priest Holme aqueduct carries the canal over the Aire. Both canal and railway have followed the river from Leeds. Here the canal goes south west into Lancashire.

Canal

226

River Aire

The Pennine Way crosses on a bridge. 250 miles long, it was the first official long distance foot path and runs from Edale in Derbyshire to Kirk Yetholm in Roxburgshire.

225   **GARGRAVE**

390 feet above sea level
Leeds 30 miles
Carlisle 83 miles

224

River Aire

223

Hellifield station was once busy with passengers and employees and it boasted two engine sheds. Many expresses and local services called here, with through trains and connections between Manchester, north Lancashire towns and the Settle and Carlisle route. In recent years the station fell into disrepair but happily was restored in 1994. It has the largest Midland Railway canopy still in existence, whose decorative ironwork features the company's initials and heraldic wyverns.

From Blackburn

Joining at Hellifield South Junction the Lancashire & Yorkshire Railway opened the line from Blackburn in 1880 when the present Hellifield station was built, replacing the original half a mile nearer to Leeds. Regular passenger services from Blackburn ceased in 1962 with the line staying open for freight and special trains.
This line is gradually being reopened.

233

LONG PRESTON

480 feet above sea level
Leeds 37½ miles
Carlisle 75½ miles

232

HELLIFIELD

520 feet above sea level
Leeds 36¼ miles
Carlisle 76¾ miles

231

All the way from Leeds the railway has followed the River Aire. Here it passes gently over the watershed to the Ribble valley which it follows up to Ribblehead.

230

229

228

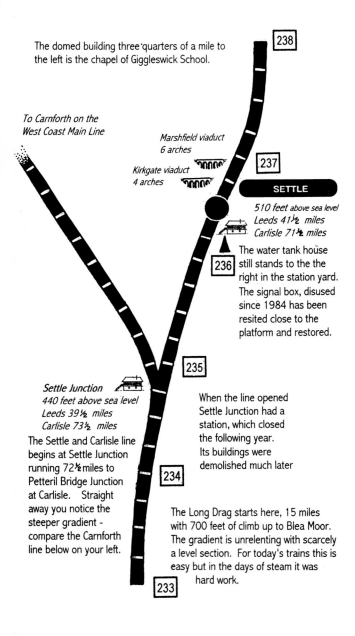

The domed building three quarters of a mile to the left is the chapel of Giggleswick School.

238

To Carnforth on the West Coast Main Line

Marshfield viaduct
6 arches

Kirkgate viaduct
4 arches

237

SETTLE

510 feet above sea level
Leeds 41½ miles
Carlisle 71½ miles

236

The water tank house still stands to the the right in the station yard. The signal box, disused since 1984 has been resited close to the platform and restored.

235

Settle Junction
440 feet above sea level
Leeds 39½ miles
Carlisle 73½ miles

The Settle and Carlisle line begins at Settle Junction running 72½ miles to Petteril Bridge Junction at Carlisle.   Straight away you notice the steeper gradient - compare the Carnforth line below on your left.

When the line opened Settle Junction had a station, which closed the following year. Its buildings were demolished much later

234

The Long Drag starts here, 15 miles with 700 feet of climb up to Blea Moor. The gradient is unrelenting with scarcely a level section. For today's trains this is easy but in the days of steam it was hard work.

233

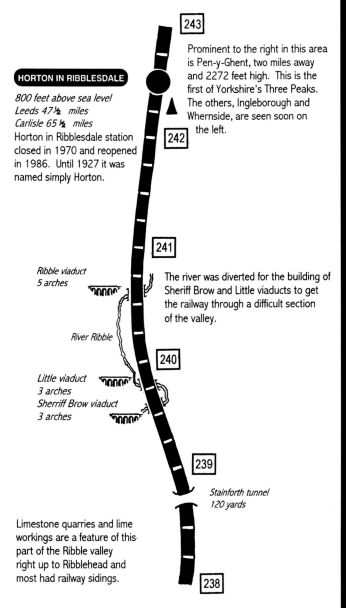

243

Prominent to the right in this area is Pen-y-Ghent, two miles away and 2272 feet high. This is the first of Yorkshire's Three Peaks. The others, Ingleborough and Whernside, are seen soon on the left.

HORTON IN RIBBLESDALE

800 feet above sea level
Leeds 47½ miles
Carlisle 65½ miles
Horton in Ribblesdale station closed in 1970 and reopened in 1986. Until 1927 it was named simply Horton.

242

241

The river was diverted for the building of Sheriff Brow and Little viaducts to get the railway through a difficult section of the valley.

Ribble viaduct
5 arches

River Ribble

240

Little viaduct
3 arches
Sherriff Brow viaduct
3 arches

239

Stainforth tunnel
120 yards

Limestone quarries and lime workings are a feature of this part of the Ribble valley right up to Ribblehead and most had railway sidings.

238

248

*Ribblehead Viaduct
24 arches*

247

RIBBLEHEAD

*1030 feet above sea level
Leeds 52¼ miles
Carlisle 60¾ miles*
Ribblehead station closed
in 1970 and reopened in
1986 for southbound trains.
Northbound trains began
stopping again in 1993 at
the new platform, which
replaced the original one
removed to build a branch
into the quarry on the left.

Ribblehead is by far the longest
viaduct on the route, taking the
railway from the Ribble valley
to cut through the mountainous
terrain towards the Eden valley.
In 1985, nearly a mile of track
was singled to reduce wear on
the viaduct and in 1989 a
waterproof membrane was laid
under the track bed, to prevent
water ingress into the arches
and piers.

246

Ingleborough, 2373 feet high
and three miles away is
prominent to the left. It is seen
well from Ribblehead viaduct.

245

During the construction period
shanty towns were built for the
workforce and their families.
Some of these were in the
Ribblehead area, below the
viaduct and around Blea Moor
tunnel, but little trace remains
of them today. A tramway
was built from the road at
Ribblehead to carry materials
for the building of Blea
Moor tunnel and parts of
its trackbed can be seen.

244

243

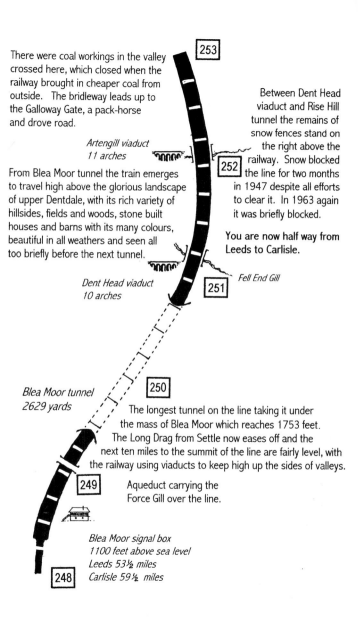

253

There were coal workings in the valley crossed here, which closed when the railway brought in cheaper coal from outside. The bridleway leads up to the Galloway Gate, a pack-horse and drove road.

Between Dent Head viaduct and Rise Hill tunnel the remains of snow fences stand on the right above the railway. Snow blocked the line for two months in 1947 despite all efforts to clear it. In 1963 again it was briefly blocked.

Artengill viaduct
11 arches

252

From Blea Moor tunnel the train emerges to travel high above the glorious landscape of upper Dentdale, with its rich variety of hillsides, fields and woods, stone built houses and barns with its many colours, beautiful in all weathers and seen all too briefly before the next tunnel.

You are now half way from Leeds to Carlisle.

Dent Head viaduct
10 arches

Fell End Gill

251

250

Blea Moor tunnel
2629 yards

The longest tunnel on the line taking it under the mass of Blea Moor which reaches 1753 feet. The Long Drag from Settle now eases off and the next ten miles to the summit of the line are fairly level, with the railway using viaducts to keep high up the sides of valleys.

249

Aqueduct carrying the Force Gill over the line.

Blea Moor signal box
1100 feet above sea level
Leeds 53½ miles
Carlisle 59½ miles

248

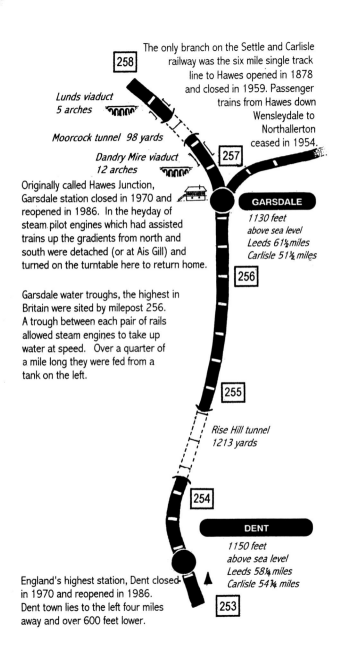

258

The only branch on the Settle and Carlisle railway was the six mile single track line to Hawes opened in 1878 and closed in 1959. Passenger trains from Hawes down Wensleydale to Northallerton ceased in 1954.

Lunds viaduct 5 arches

Moorcock tunnel 98 yards

Dandry Mire viaduct 12 arches

257

GARSDALE
1130 feet above sea level
Leeds 61½ miles
Carlisle 51½ miles

Originally called Hawes Junction, Garsdale station closed in 1970 and reopened in 1986. In the heyday of steam pilot engines which had assisted trains up the gradients from north and south were detached (or at Ais Gill) and turned on the turntable here to return home.

256

Garsdale water troughs, the highest in Britain were sited by milepost 256. A trough between each pair of rails allowed steam engines to take up water at speed. Over a quarter of a mile long they were fed from a tank on the left.

255

Rise Hill tunnel 1213 yards

254

DENT
1150 feet above sea level
Leeds 58¼ miles
Carlisle 54¾ miles

England's highest station, Dent closed in 1970 and reopened in 1986. Dent town lies to the left four miles away and over 600 feet lower.

253

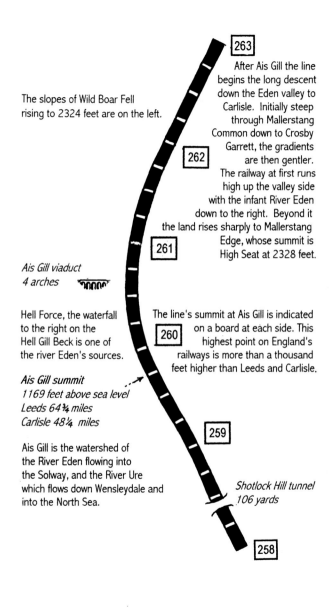

263

After Ais Gill the line begins the long descent down the Eden valley to Carlisle. Initially steep through Mallerstang Common down to Crosby Garrett, the gradients are then gentler. The railway at first runs high up the valley side with the infant River Eden down to the right. Beyond it the land rises sharply to Mallerstang Edge, whose summit is High Seat at 2328 feet.

The slopes of Wild Boar Fell rising to 2324 feet are on the left.

262

261

Ais Gill viaduct
4 arches

Hell Force, the waterfall to the right on the Hell Gill Beck is one of the river Eden's sources.

The line's summit at Ais Gill is indicated on a board at each side. This highest point on England's railways is more than a thousand feet higher than Leeds and Carlisle.

260

Ais Gill summit
1169 feet above sea level
Leeds 64¾ miles
Carlisle 48¼ miles

Ais Gill is the watershed of the River Eden flowing into the Solway, and the River Ure which flows down Wensleydale and into the North Sea.

259

Shotlock Hill tunnel
106 yards

258

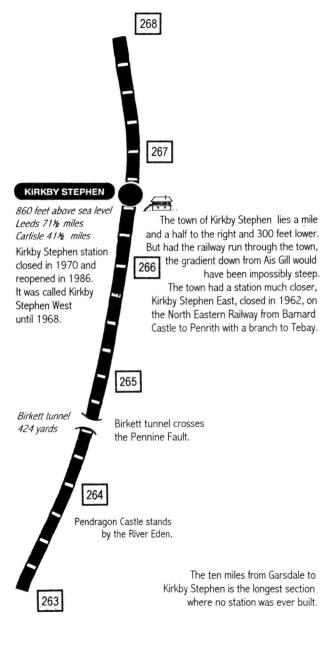

268

267

KIRKBY STEPHEN

860 feet above sea level
Leeds 71½ miles
Carlisle 41½ miles
Kirkby Stephen station
closed in 1970 and
reopened in 1986.
It was called Kirkby
Stephen West
until 1968.

The town of Kirkby Stephen lies a mile
and a half to the right and 300 feet lower.
But had the railway run through the town,
the gradient down from Ais Gill would
have been impossibly steep.
The town had a station much closer,
Kirkby Stephen East, closed in 1962, on
the North Eastern Railway from Barnard
Castle to Penrith with a branch to Tebay.

266

265

Birkett tunnel
424 yards

Birkett tunnel crosses
the Pennine Fault.

264

Pendragon Castle stands
by the River Eden.

The ten miles from Garsdale to
Kirkby Stephen is the longest section
where no station was ever built.

263

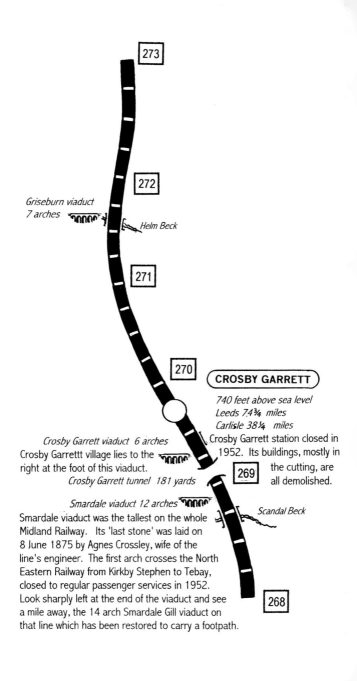

273

272

Griseburn viaduct
7 arches 🏛 ⌐ Helm Beck

271

270

(CROSBY GARRETT)

740 feet above sea level
Leeds 74¾ miles
Carlisle 38¼ miles
Crosby Garrett station closed in
1952. Its buildings, mostly in
the cutting, are
all demolished.

Crosby Garrett viaduct 6 arches
Crosby Garrettt village lies to the 🏛
right at the foot of this viaduct.
Crosby Garrett tunnel 181 yards

269

Smardale viaduct 12 arches 🏛
Smardale viaduct was the tallest on the whole
Midland Railway. Its 'last stone' was laid on
8 June 1875 by Agnes Crossley, wife of the
line's engineer. The first arch crosses the North
Eastern Railway from Kirkby Stephen to Tebay,
closed to regular passenger services in 1952.
Look sharply left at the end of the viaduct and see
a mile away, the 14 arch Smardale Gill viaduct on
that line which has been restored to carry a footpath.

Scandal Beck

268

278

Connection to the North Eastern Railway from Penrith to Barnard Castle, which closed to regular passenger services in 1962. Appleby East station on that line was a hundred yards up the road from here.

Appleby North Junction

APPLEBY

520 feet above sea level
Leeds 82¼ miles
Carlisle 30¾ miles
The station was called Appleby West from 1952 to 1968.

277

The water tank and column on the Leeds bound platform were reinstated in 1991.

Displaying the slogan 'Milk for London' the dairy on the right had a siding from 1930 to 1970, where trains of milk tankers started their journey south.

276

Just before the station, on the left in the Midland Railway goods shed and goods yard, the Appleby Heritage Centre was set up in 1997, to provide employment training, including work on repairing items of railway interest.

Ormside viaduct
10 arches

ORMSIDE

River Eden

275

520 feet above sea level
Leeds 79¾ miles
Carlisle 33¼ miles
Ormside station closed in 1952 and buildings remain on the left.

274

Helm tunnel
571 yards

273

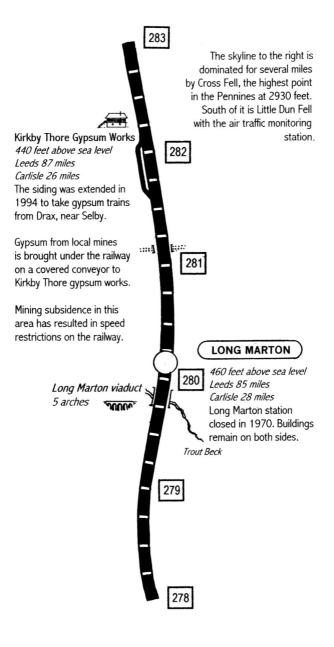

283

The skyline to the right is dominated for several miles by Cross Fell, the highest point in the Pennines at 2930 feet. South of it is Little Dun Fell with the air traffic monitoring station.

Kirkby Thore Gypsum Works
440 feet above sea level
Leeds 87 miles
Carlisle 26 miles
The siding was extended in 1994 to take gypsum trains from Drax, near Selby.

282

Gypsum from local mines is brought under the railway on a covered conveyor to Kirkby Thore gypsum works.

281

Mining subsidence in this area has resulted in speed restrictions on the railway.

(**LONG MARTON**)

Long Marton viaduct
5 arches

280

460 feet above sea level
Leeds 85 miles
Carlisle 28 miles
Long Marton station closed in 1970. Buildings remain on both sides.

Trout Beck

279

278

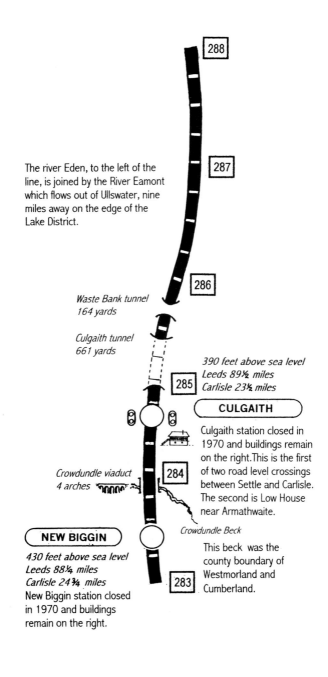

288

287

The river Eden, to the left of the line, is joined by the River Eamont which flows out of Ullswater, nine miles away on the edge of the Lake District.

286

Waste Bank tunnel 164 yards

Culgaith tunnel 661 yards

390 feet above sea level
Leeds 89½ miles
Carlisle 23½ miles

285

CULGAITH

Culgaith station closed in 1970 and buildings remain on the right. This is the first of two road level crossings between Settle and Carlisle. The second is Low House near Armathwaite.

Crowdundle viaduct 4 arches

284

Crowdundle Beck

This beck was the county boundary of Westmorland and Cumberland.

NEW BIGGIN

430 feet above sea level
Leeds 88¼ miles
Carlisle 24¾ miles
New Biggin station closed in 1970 and buildings remain on the right.

283

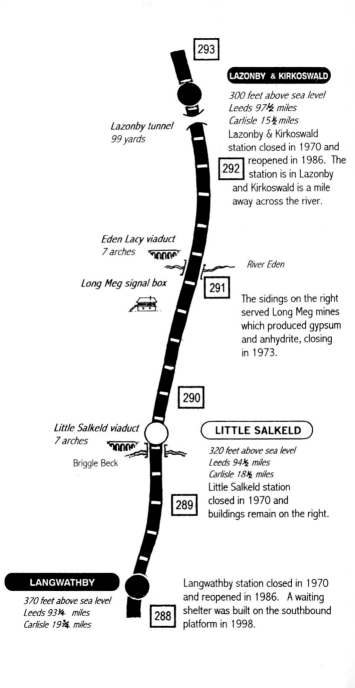

293

LAZONBY & KIRKOSWALD

300 feet above sea level
Leeds 97½ miles
Carlisle 15½ miles
Lazonby & Kirkoswald
station closed in 1970 and
reopened in 1986. The
station is in Lazonby
and Kirkoswald is a mile
away across the river.

292

Lazonby tunnel
99 yards

Eden Lacy viaduct
7 arches

River Eden

Long Meg signal box

291

The sidings on the right
served Long Meg mines
which produced gypsum
and anhydrite, closing
in 1973.

290

Little Salkeld viaduct
7 arches

LITTLE SALKELD

320 feet above sea level
Leeds 94½ miles
Carlisle 18½ miles
Little Salkeld station
closed in 1970 and
buildings remain on the right.

Briggle Beck

289

LANGWATHBY

370 feet above sea level
Leeds 93¼ miles
Carlisle 19¾ miles

288

Langwathby station closed in 1970
and reopened in 1986. A waiting
shelter was built on the southbound
platform in 1998.

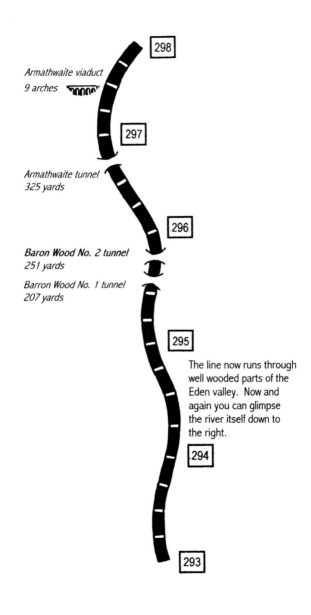

298

Armathwaite viaduct
9 arches

297

Armathwaite tunnel
325 yards

296

Baron Wood No. 2 tunnel
251 yards

Barron Wood No. 1 tunnel
207 yards

295

The line now runs through
well wooded parts of the
Eden valley. Now and
again you can glimpse
the river itself down to
the right.

294

293

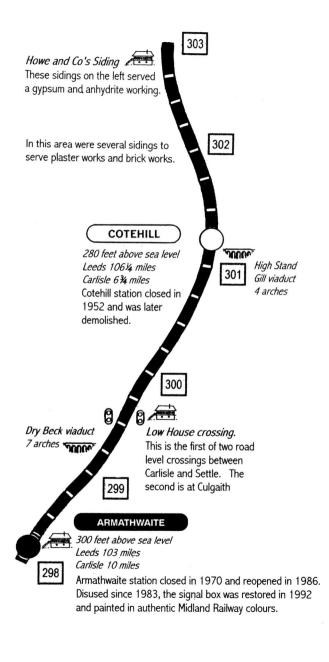

303

Howe and Co's Siding
These sidings on the left served
a gypsum and anhydrite working.

In this area were several sidings to
serve plaster works and brick works.

302

COTEHILL

280 feet above sea level
Leeds 106¼ miles
Carlisle 6¾ miles
Cotehill station closed in
1952 and was later
demolished.

301 *High Stand*
Gill viaduct
4 arches

300

Dry Beck viaduct
7 arches

Low House crossing.
This is the first of two road
level crossings between
Carlisle and Settle. The
second is at Culgaith

299

ARMATHWAITE

300 feet above sea level
Leeds 103 miles
Carlisle 10 miles

298

Armathwaite station closed in 1970 and reopened in 1986.
Disused since 1983, the signal box was restored in 1992
and painted in authentic Midland Railway colours.

CARLISLE

70 feet above sea level
Leeds 113 miles

London Road Junction
to West Coast Main Line

Petteril Bridge Junction

The Settle and Carlisle
Railway ends at Petteril
Bridge Junction, where it joins
the former North Eastern
Railway line from Newcastle.
The narrow River Petteril is
crossed immediately.
Durran Hill engine shed stood to
the left and Durran Hill sidings
lay on both sides of the line for
nearly half a mile. Little trace
of these is seen today.

307

Carlisle Citadel station opened in 1847
and was extended later. With the arrival
of the Midland from Settle there were
seven railway companies sharing it, the
largest number for any British station.
They were: Caledonian, Midland,
Glasgow & South Western, London &
North Western, Maryport & Carlisle,
North British and North Eastern
Companies.

From Newcastle

SCOTBY

140 feet above sea level
Leeds 110¾ miles
Carlisle 2¾ miles

Scotby station closed in
1942 and buildings on
the left. Scotby also
had a station on the
Carlisle-Newcastle
line which closed
in 1959.

306

305

304

CUMWHINTON

200 feet above sea level
Leeds 109 miles
Carlisle 4 miles

Cumwhinton station closed
in 1956 and buildings
remain on both sides.

303

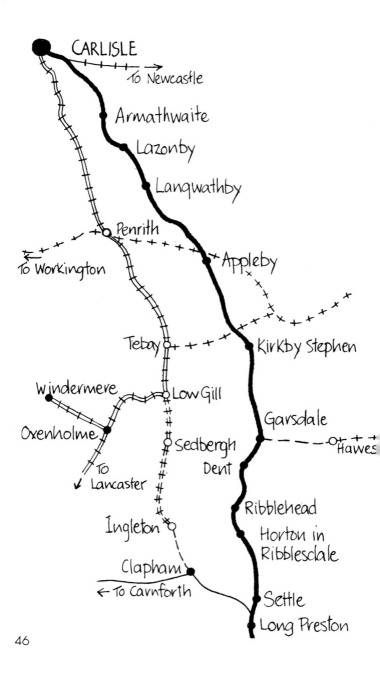

CARLISLE

To Newcastle

Armathwaite

Lazonby

Langwathby

Penrith

To Workington

Appleby

Tebay

Kirkby Stephen

Windermere

Low Gill

Oxenholme

Garsdale

Hawes

Sedbergh

To
Lancaster

Dent

Ingleton

Ribblehead

Horton in
Ribblesdale

Clapham

← To Carnforth

Settle

Long Preston

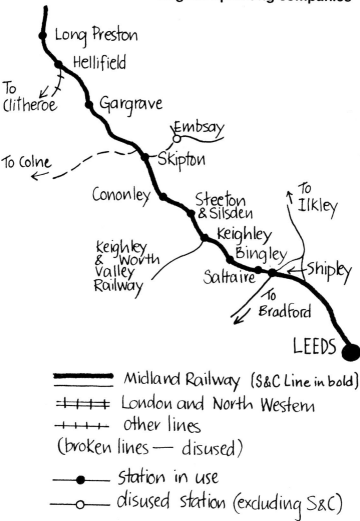

Map of the Leeds–Settle–Carlisle and associated lines showing original operating companies

Long Preston
Hellifield
To Clitheroe
Gargrave
Embsay
To Colne
Skipton
Cononley
Steeton & Silsden
Keighley
To Ilkley
Keighley & Worth Valley Railway
Bingley
Saltaire
Shipley
To Bradford
LEEDS

━━━━ Midland Railway (S&C Line in bold)
╪┼┼┼╪ London and North Western
┼┼┼┼ other lines
(broken lines — disused)

──●── station in use
──○── disused station (excluding S&C)

Trains on this route originally used Leeds Wellington station, modernised in 1938 with an elegant concourse and linked to the adjacent Leeds New station to become Leeds City. This concourse, not used for passengers since 1966, has been restored for passengers again in the current regeneration work.

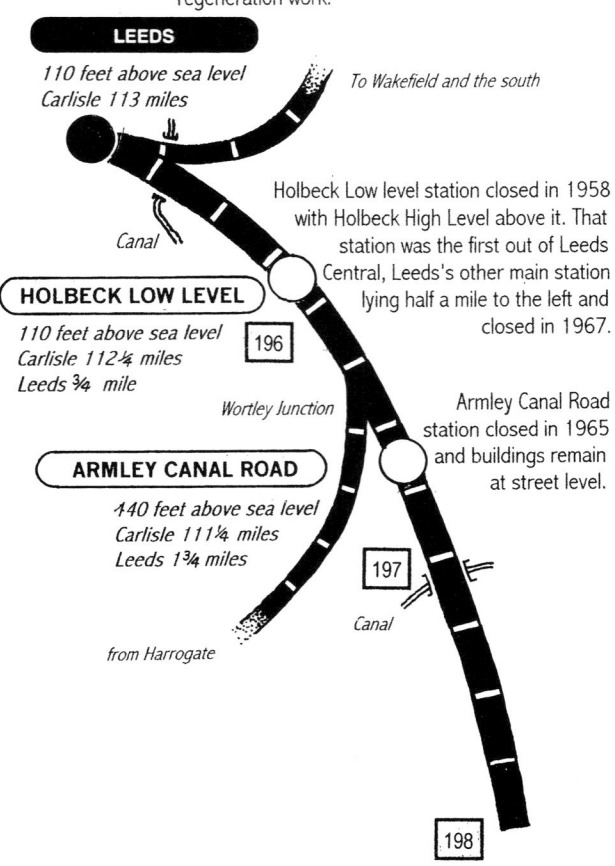

LEEDS

110 feet above sea level
Carlisle 113 miles

To Wakefield and the south

Canal

Holbeck Low level station closed in 1958 with Holbeck High Level above it. That station was the first out of Leeds Central, Leeds's other main station lying half a mile to the left and closed in 1967.

HOLBECK LOW LEVEL

110 feet above sea level
Carlisle 112¼ miles
Leeds ¾ mile

196

Wortley Junction

Armley Canal Road station closed in 1965 and buildings remain at street level.

ARMLEY CANAL ROAD

140 feet above sea level
Carlisle 111¼ miles
Leeds 1¾ miles

197

Canal

from Harrogate

198

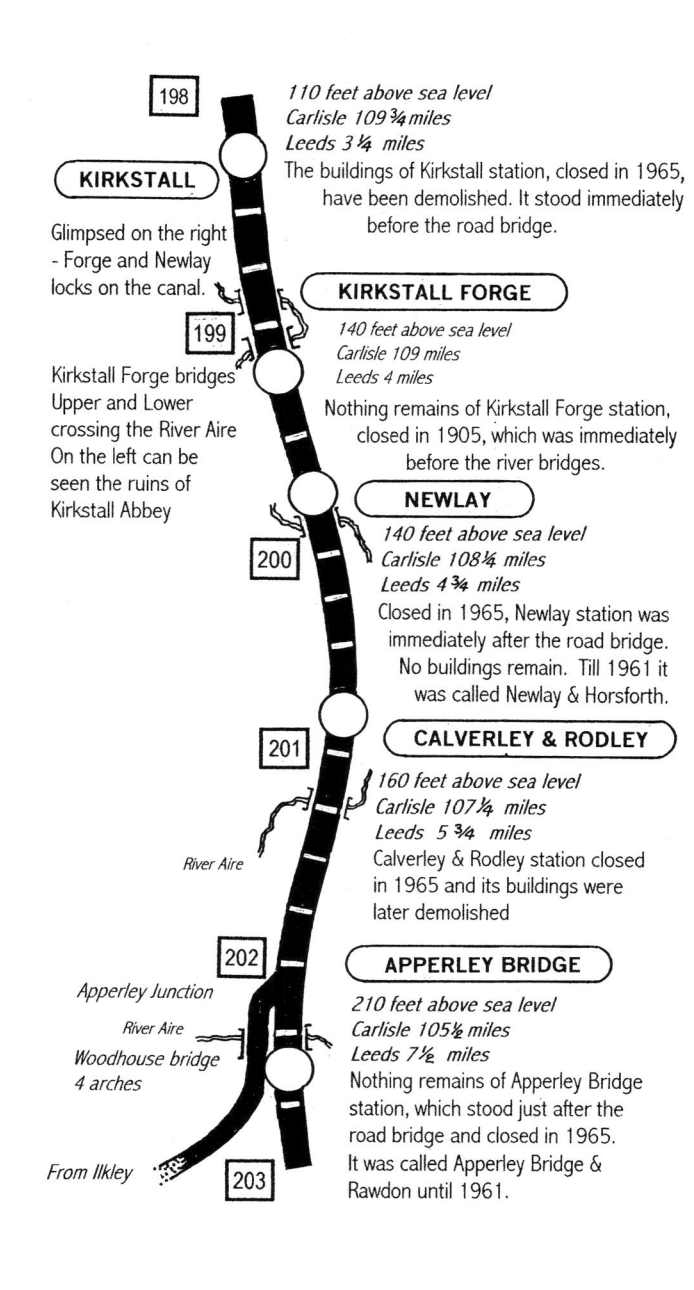

198

110 feet above sea level
Carlisle 109 ¾ miles
Leeds 3 ¼ miles
The buildings of Kirkstall station, closed in 1965,
have been demolished. It stood immediately
before the road bridge.

KIRKSTALL

Glimpsed on the right
- Forge and Newlay
locks on the canal.

KIRKSTALL FORGE

140 feet above sea level
Carlisle 109 miles
Leeds 4 miles

Nothing remains of Kirkstall Forge station,
closed in 1905, which was immediately
before the river bridges.

199

Kirkstall Forge bridges
Upper and Lower
crossing the River Aire
On the left can be
seen the ruins of
Kirkstall Abbey

NEWLAY

140 feet above sea level
Carlisle 108 ¼ miles
Leeds 4 ¾ miles
Closed in 1965, Newlay station was
immediately after the road bridge.
No buildings remain. Till 1961 it
was called Newlay & Horsforth.

200

CALVERLEY & RODLEY

160 feet above sea level
Carlisle 107 ¼ miles
Leeds 5 ¾ miles
Calverley & Rodley station closed
in 1965 and its buildings were
later demolished

201

River Aire

202

Apperley Junction

River Aire
Woodhouse bridge
4 arches

APPERLEY BRIDGE

210 feet above sea level
Carlisle 105 ½ miles
Leeds 7 ½ miles
Nothing remains of Apperley Bridge
station, which stood just after the
road bridge and closed in 1965.
It was called Apperley Bridge &
Rawdon until 1961.

From Ilkley

203

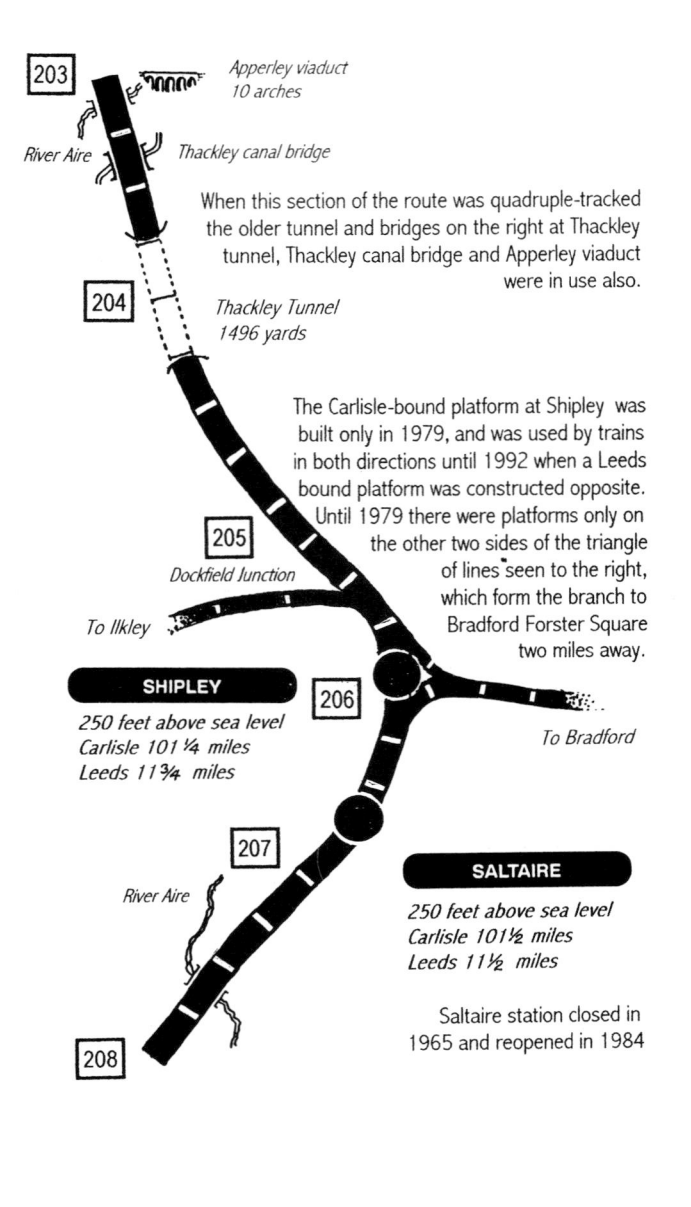

203

*Apperley viaduct
10 arches*

River Aire

Thackley canal bridge

When this section of the route was quadruple-tracked
the older tunnel and bridges on the right at Thackley
tunnel, Thackley canal bridge and Apperley viaduct
were in use also.

204

*Thackley Tunnel
1496 yards*

The Carlisle-bound platform at Shipley was
built only in 1979, and was used by trains
in both directions until 1992 when a Leeds
bound platform was constructed opposite.
Until 1979 there were platforms only on
the other two sides of the triangle
of lines seen to the right,
which form the branch to
Bradford Forster Square
two miles away.

205

Dockfield Junction

To Ilkley

SHIPLEY

*250 feet above sea level
Carlisle 101 ¼ miles
Leeds 11 ¾ miles*

206

To Bradford

207

River Aire

SALTAIRE

*250 feet above sea level
Carlisle 101½ miles
Leeds 11½ miles*

Saltaire station closed in
1965 and reopened in 1984

208

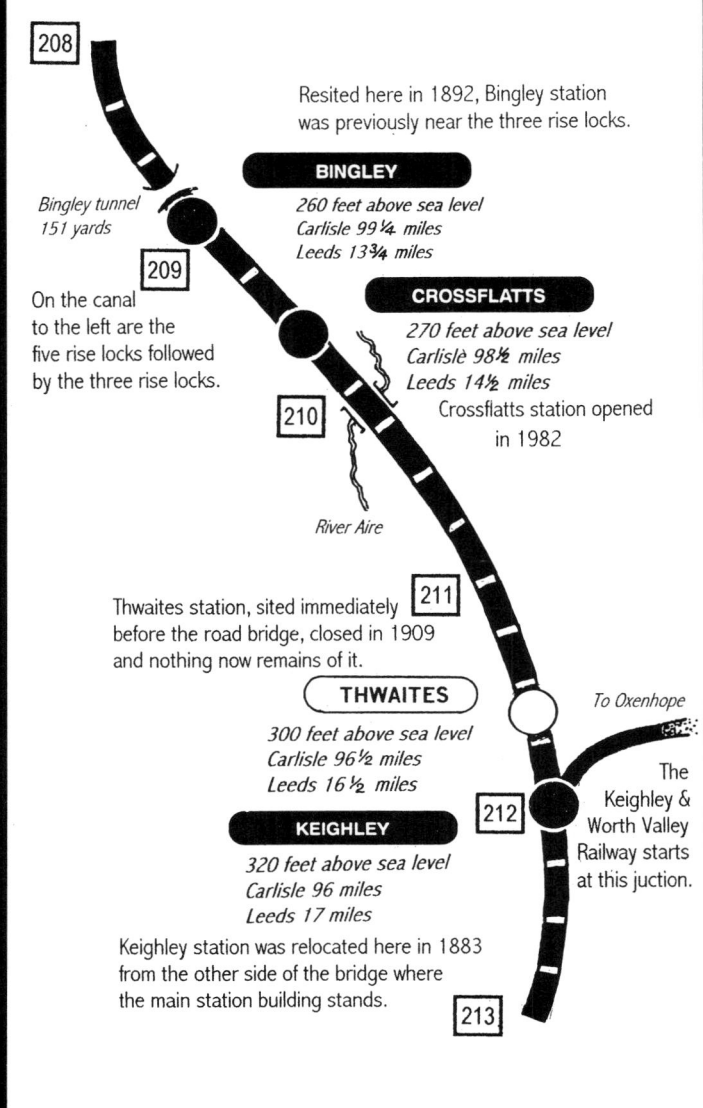

208

209

210

211

212

213

Resited here in 1892, Bingley station was previously near the three rise locks.

Bingley tunnel
151 yards

BINGLEY

260 feet above sea level
Carlisle 99 ¼ miles
Leeds 13 ¾ miles

CROSSFLATTS

270 feet above sea level
Carlislè 98 ½ miles
Leeds 14 ½ miles
Crossflatts station opened
in 1982

On the canal to the left are the five rise locks followed by the three rise locks.

River Aire

Thwaites station, sited immediately before the road bridge, closed in 1909 and nothing now remains of it.

THWAITES

300 feet above sea level
Carlisle 96 ½ miles
Leeds 16 ½ miles

To Oxenhope

The Keighley & Worth Valley Railway starts at this juction.

KEIGHLEY

320 feet above sea level
Carlisle 96 miles
Leeds 17 miles

Keighley station was relocated here in 1883 from the other side of the bridge where the main station building stands.

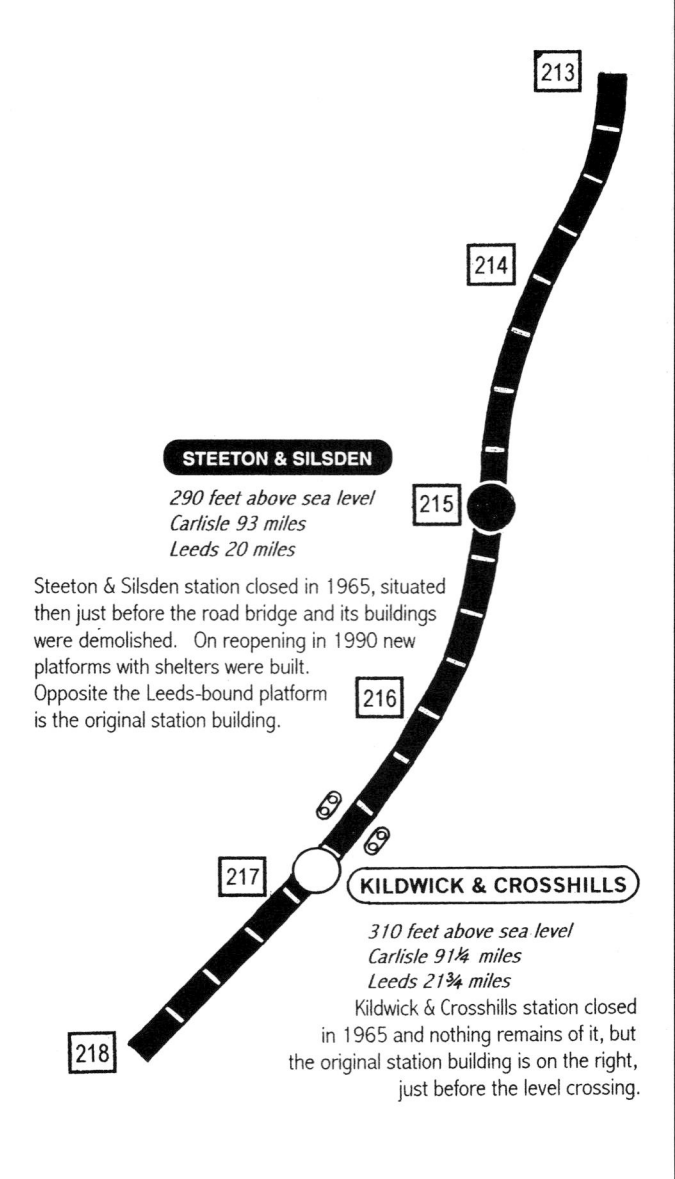

STEETON & SILSDEN

290 feet above sea level
Carlisle 93 miles
Leeds 20 miles

Steeton & Silsden station closed in 1965, situated
then just before the road bridge and its buildings
were demolished.   On reopening in 1990 new
platforms with shelters were built.
Opposite the Leeds-bound platform
is the original station building.

KILDWICK & CROSSHILLS

310 feet above sea level
Carlisle 91¼ miles
Leeds 21¾ miles
Kildwick & Crosshills station closed
in 1965 and nothing remains of it, but
the original station building is on the right,
just before the level crossing.

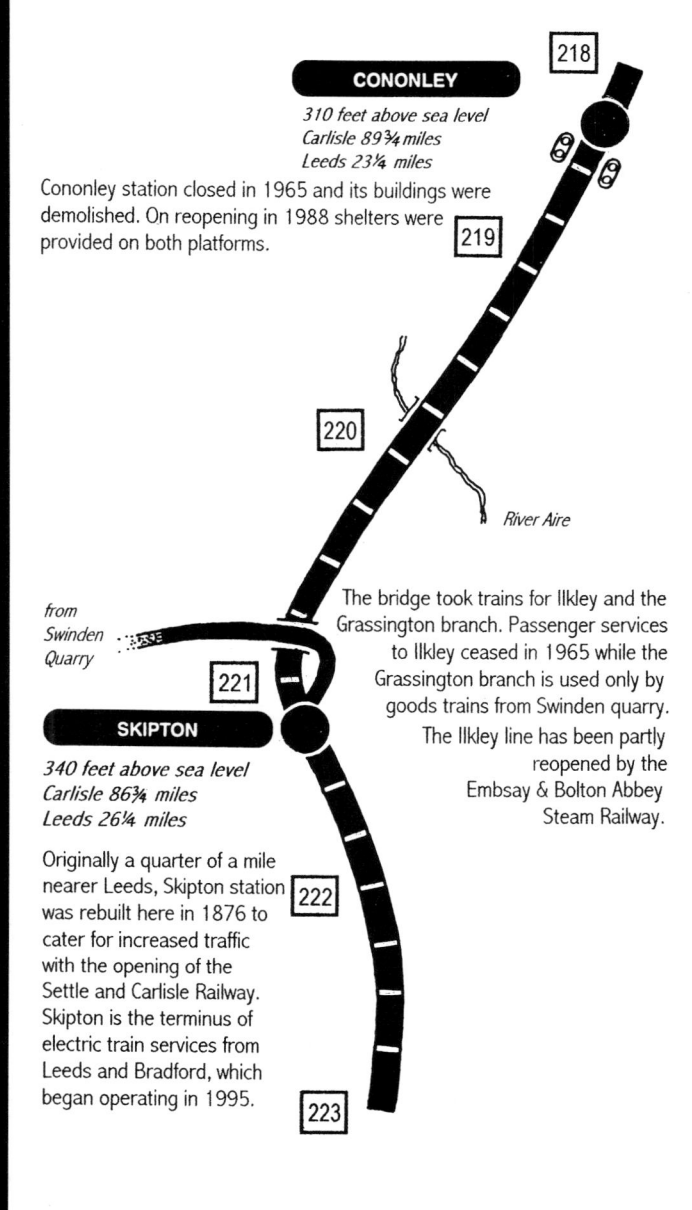

218

CONONLEY

310 feet above sea level
Carlisle 89¾ miles
Leeds 23¼ miles

Cononley station closed in 1965 and its buildings were demolished. On reopening in 1988 shelters were provided on both platforms.

219

220

River Aire

from Swinden Quarry

221

SKIPTON

340 feet above sea level
Carlisle 86¾ miles
Leeds 26¼ miles

Originally a quarter of a mile nearer Leeds, Skipton station was rebuilt here in 1876 to cater for increased traffic with the opening of the Settle and Carlisle Railway. Skipton is the terminus of electric train services from Leeds and Bradford, which began operating in 1995.

The bridge took trains for Ilkley and the Grassington branch. Passenger services to Ilkley ceased in 1965 while the Grassington branch is used only by goods trains from Swinden quarry.

The Ilkley line has been partly reopened by the Embsay & Bolton Abbey Steam Railway.

222

223

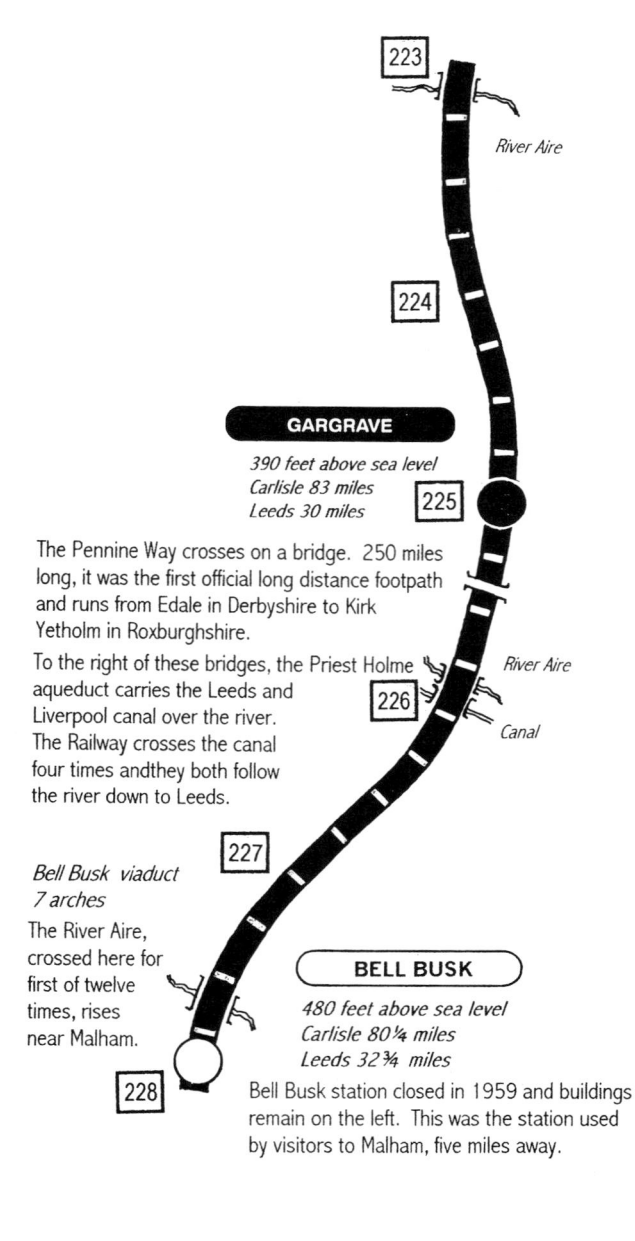

| 223 |

River Aire

| 224 |

GARGRAVE

390 feet above sea level
Carlisle 83 miles
Leeds 30 miles

| 225 |

The Pennine Way crosses on a bridge. 250 miles long, it was the first official long distance footpath and runs from Edale in Derbyshire to Kirk Yetholm in Roxburghshire.

To the right of these bridges, the Priest Holme aqueduct carries the Leeds and Liverpool canal over the river. The Railway crosses the canal four times andthey both follow the river down to Leeds.

| 226 |

River Aire

Canal

| 227 |

Bell Busk viaduct
7 arches

The River Aire, crossed here for first of twelve times, rises near Malham.

BELL BUSK

480 feet above sea level
Carlisle 80¼ miles
Leeds 32¾ miles

| 228 |

Bell Busk station closed in 1959 and buildings remain on the left. This was the station used by visitors to Malham, five miles away.

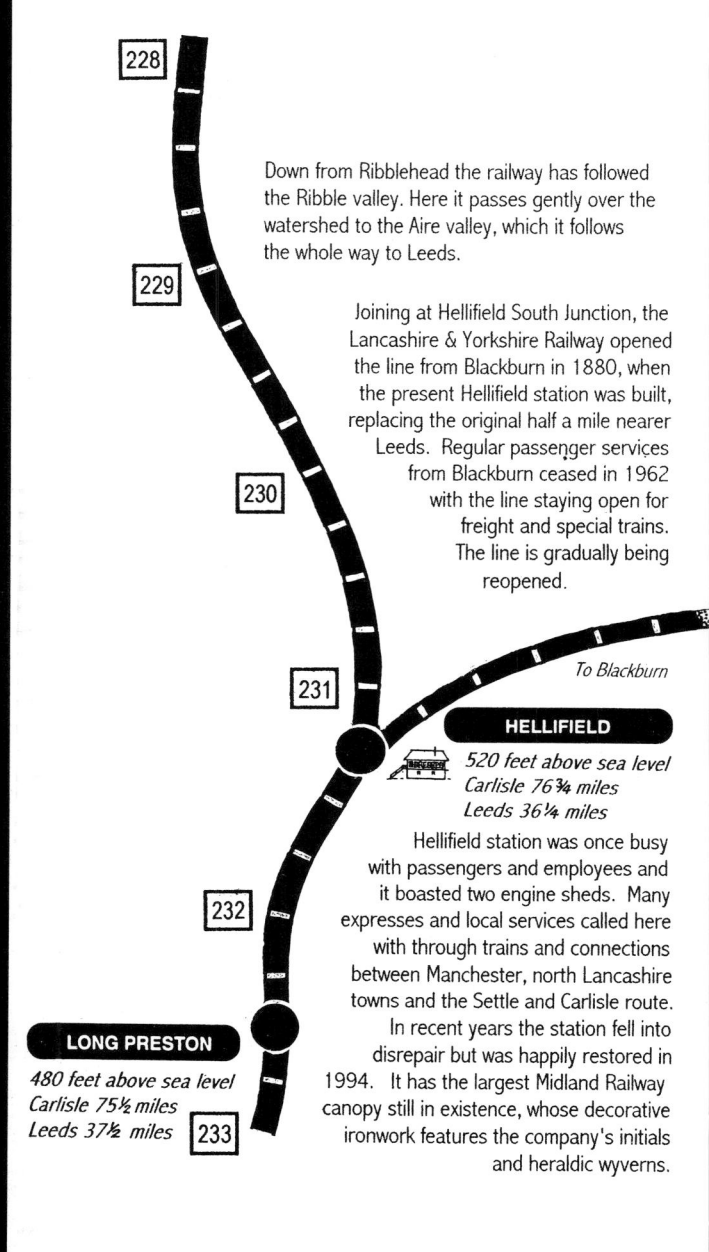

228

229

230

Down from Ribblehead the railway has followed the Ribble valley. Here it passes gently over the watershed to the Aire valley, which it follows the whole way to Leeds.

Joining at Hellifield South Junction, the Lancashire & Yorkshire Railway opened the line from Blackburn in 1880, when the present Hellifield station was built, replacing the original half a mile nearer Leeds. Regular passenger services from Blackburn ceased in 1962 with the line staying open for freight and special trains. The line is gradually being reopened.

To Blackburn

231

HELLIFIELD

*520 feet above sea level
Carlisle 76¾ miles
Leeds 36¼ miles*

Hellifield station was once busy with passengers and employees and it boasted two engine sheds. Many expresses and local services called here with through trains and connections between Manchester, north Lancashire towns and the Settle and Carlisle route. In recent years the station fell into disrepair but was happily restored in 1994. It has the largest Midland Railway canopy still in existence, whose decorative ironwork features the company's initials and heraldic wyverns.

232

LONG PRESTON

*480 feet above sea level
Carlisle 75½ miles
Leeds 37½ miles*

233

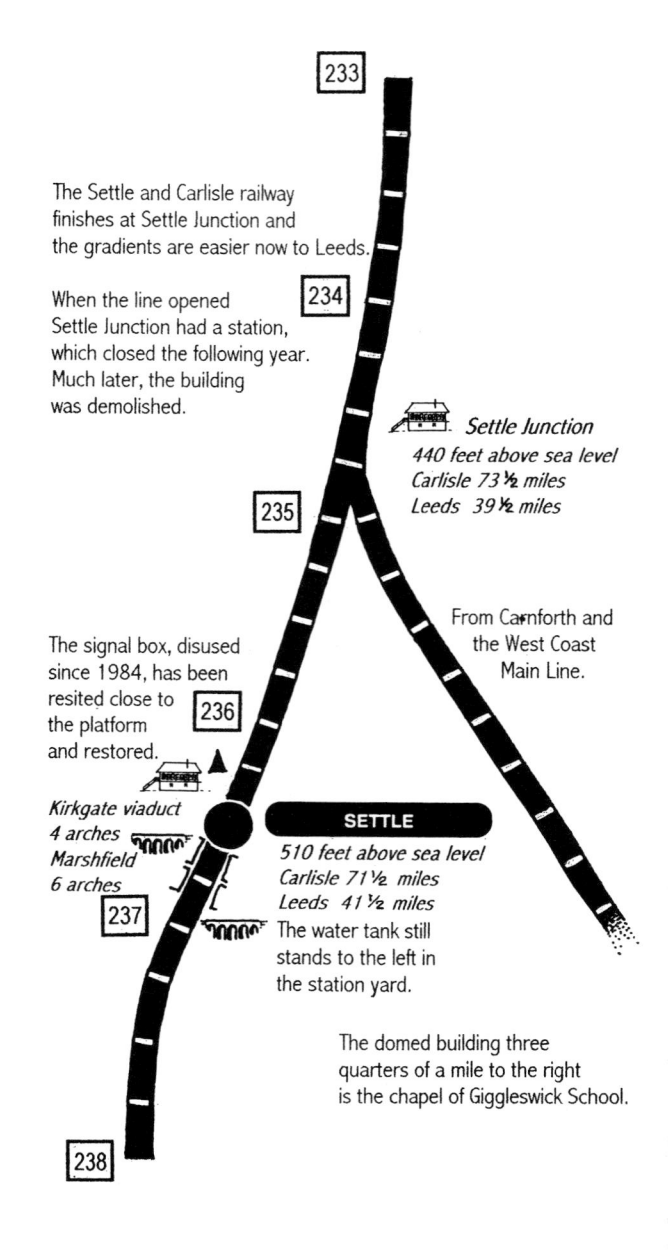

233

The Settle and Carlisle railway
finishes at Settle Junction and
the gradients are easier now to Leeds.

234

When the line opened
Settle Junction had a station,
which closed the following year.
Much later, the building
was demolished.

Settle Junction
440 feet above sea level
Carlisle 73 ½ miles
Leeds 39 ½ miles

235

From Carnforth and
the West Coast
Main Line.

The signal box, disused
since 1984, has been
resited close to
the platform
and restored.

236

Kirkgate viaduct
4 arches
Marshfield
6 arches

237

SETTLE

510 feet above sea level
Carlisle 71 ½ miles
Leeds 41 ½ miles
The water tank still
stands to the left in
the station yard.

The domed building three
quarters of a mile to the right
is the chapel of Giggleswick School.

238

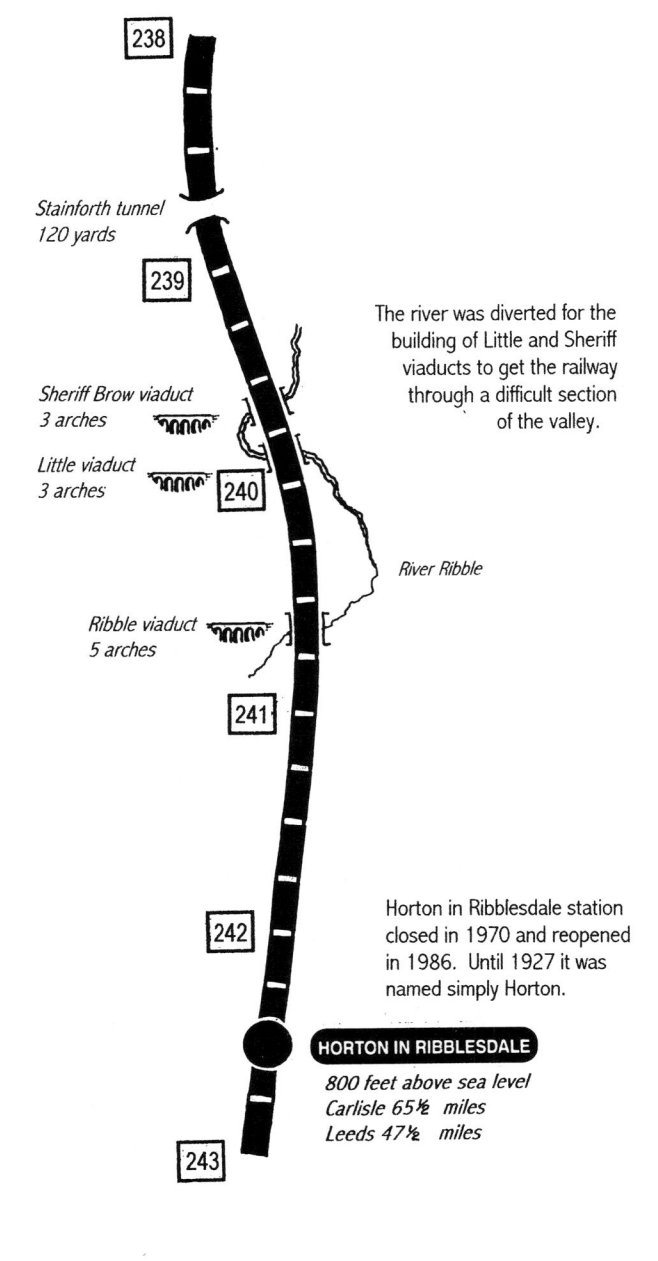

238

*Stainforth tunnel
120 yards*

239

*Sheriff Brow viaduct
3 arches*

*Little viaduct
3 arches*

240

*Ribble viaduct
5 arches*

241

242

243

The river was diverted for the building of Little and Sheriff viaducts to get the railway through a difficult section of the valley.

River Ribble

Horton in Ribblesdale station closed in 1970 and reopened in 1986. Until 1927 it was named simply Horton.

HORTON IN RIBBLESDALE

*800 feet above sea level
Carlisle 65½ miles
Leeds 47½ miles*

243

Prominent on the left
in this area is Pen-y-Ghent
three miles away and
2272 feet high

244

Limestone quarries and lime
workings are a feature of the
Ribble valley down nearly
as far as Settle, and most
had railway sidings

245

During the railway construction period,
shanty towns were built for the workforce
and their families. Some of these were
around Blea Moor tunnel and below
Ribblehead viaduct and beyond, but little
trace remains of these today. A tramway
was builtfrom the road at Ribblehead to
carry materials for the building of Blea
Moor tunnel, and parts of its trackbed
can still be seen.

246

Ribblehead station closed in 1970 and
reopened in 1986 for southbound trains.
Northbound trains began stopping again
in 1993 at the new platform which
replaced the original one removed to build
a branch into the quarry on the right.

Ribblehead is by far the
longest viaduct on the route,
taking the railway from
the mountainous section
to run down the Ribble
valley. In 1985 nearly a
mile of track was singled to
reduce wear on the viaduct,
and in 1989 a waterproof membrane
was laid under the track bed, to prevent
water ingress into the arches and piers.

247

RIBBLEHEAD

1030 feet above sea level
Carlisle 60¾ miles
Leeds 52¼ miles

Ribblehead Viaduct
24 arches

248

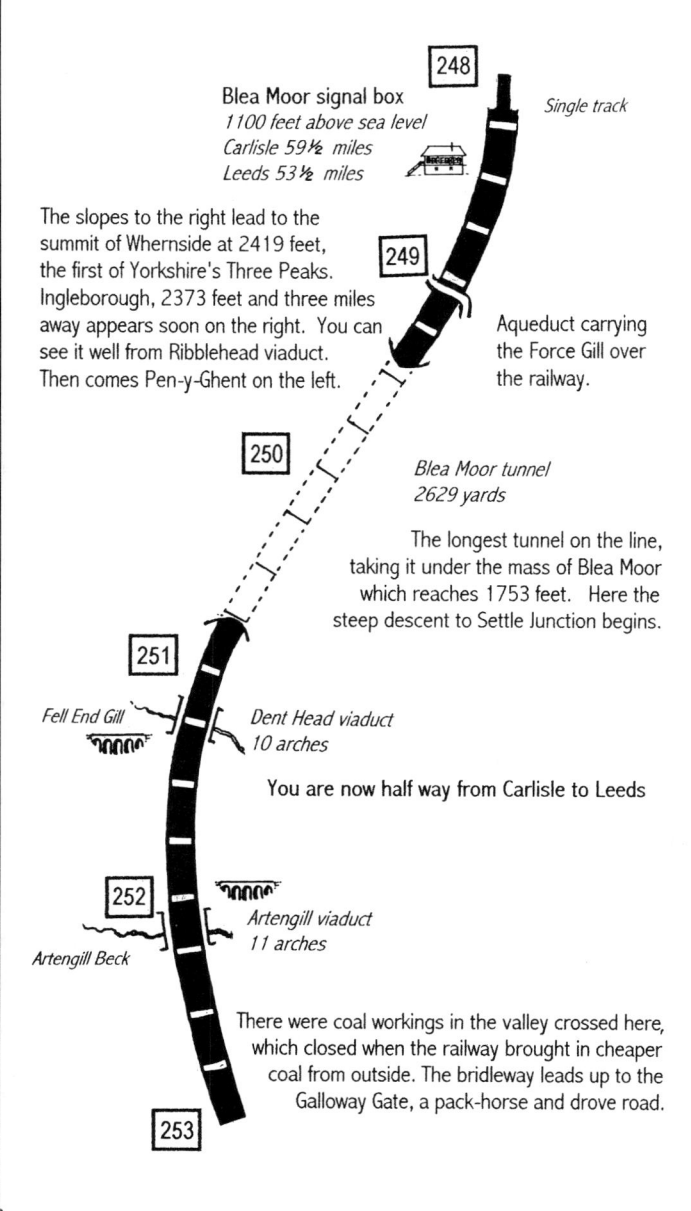

248

Blea Moor signal box
1100 feet above sea level
Carlisle 59½ miles
Leeds 53½ miles

Single track

The slopes to the right lead to the summit of Whernside at 2419 feet, the first of Yorkshire's Three Peaks. Ingleborough, 2373 feet and three miles away appears soon on the right. You can see it well from Ribblehead viaduct. Then comes Pen-y-Ghent on the left.

249

Aqueduct carrying the Force Gill over the railway.

250

Blea Moor tunnel
2629 yards

The longest tunnel on the line, taking it under the mass of Blea Moor which reaches 1753 feet. Here the steep descent to Settle Junction begins.

251

Fell End Gill

Dent Head viaduct
10 arches

You are now half way from Carlisle to Leeds

252

Artengill viaduct
11 arches

Artengill Beck

There were coal workings in the valley crossed here, which closed when the railway brought in cheaper coal from outside. The bridleway leads up to the Galloway Gate, a pack-horse and drove road.

253

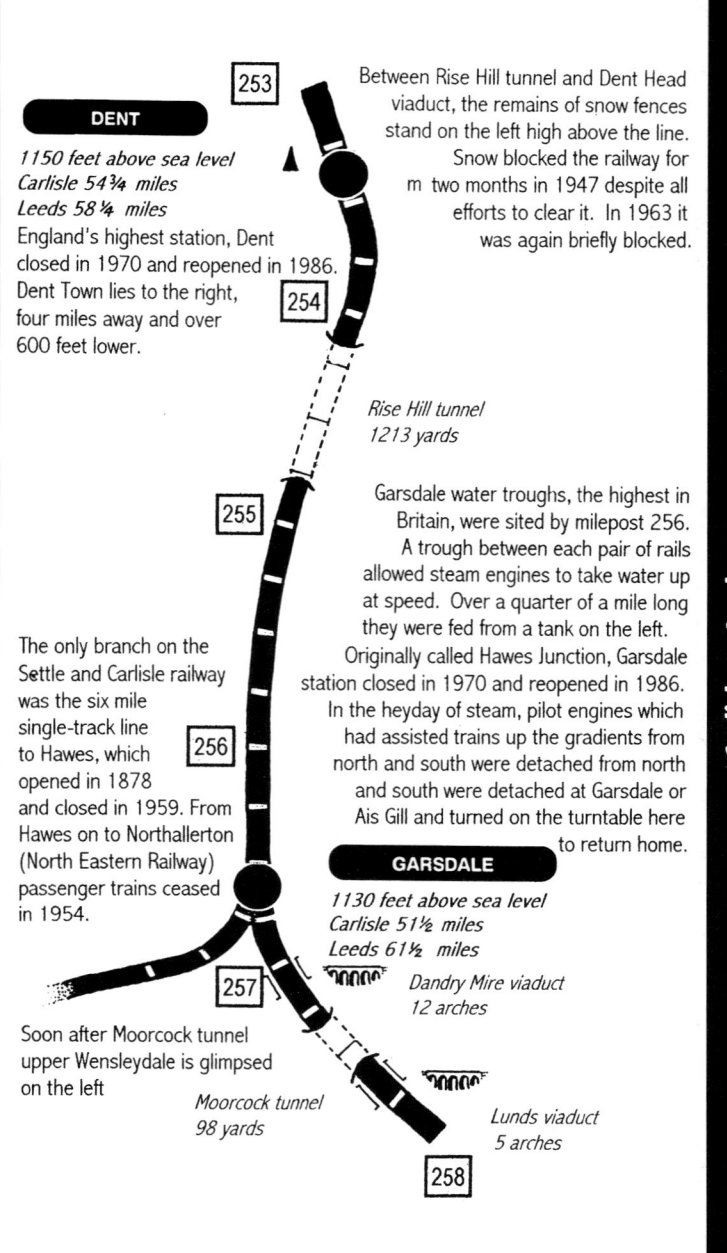

DENT

1150 feet above sea level
Carlisle 54¾ miles
Leeds 58¼ miles
England's highest station, Dent closed in 1970 and reopened in 1986. Dent Town lies to the right, four miles away and over 600 feet lower.

Between Rise Hill tunnel and Dent Head viaduct, the remains of snow fences stand on the left high above the line. Snow blocked the railway for m two months in 1947 despite all efforts to clear it. In 1963 it was again briefly blocked.

Rise Hill tunnel
1213 yards

Garsdale water troughs, the highest in Britain, were sited by milepost 256. A trough between each pair of rails allowed steam engines to take water up at speed. Over a quarter of a mile long they were fed from a tank on the left. Originally called Hawes Junction, Garsdale station closed in 1970 and reopened in 1986. In the heyday of steam, pilot engines which had assisted trains up the gradients from north and south were detached from north and south were detached at Garsdale or Ais Gill and turned on the turntable here to return home.

The only branch on the Settle and Carlisle railway was the six mile single-track line to Hawes, which opened in 1878 and closed in 1959. From Hawes on to Northallerton (North Eastern Railway) passenger trains ceased in 1954.

GARSDALE

1130 feet above sea level
Carlisle 51½ miles
Leeds 61½ miles

Dandry Mire viaduct
12 arches

Soon after Moorcock tunnel upper Wensleydale is glimpsed on the left

Moorcock tunnel
98 yards

Lunds viaduct
5 arches

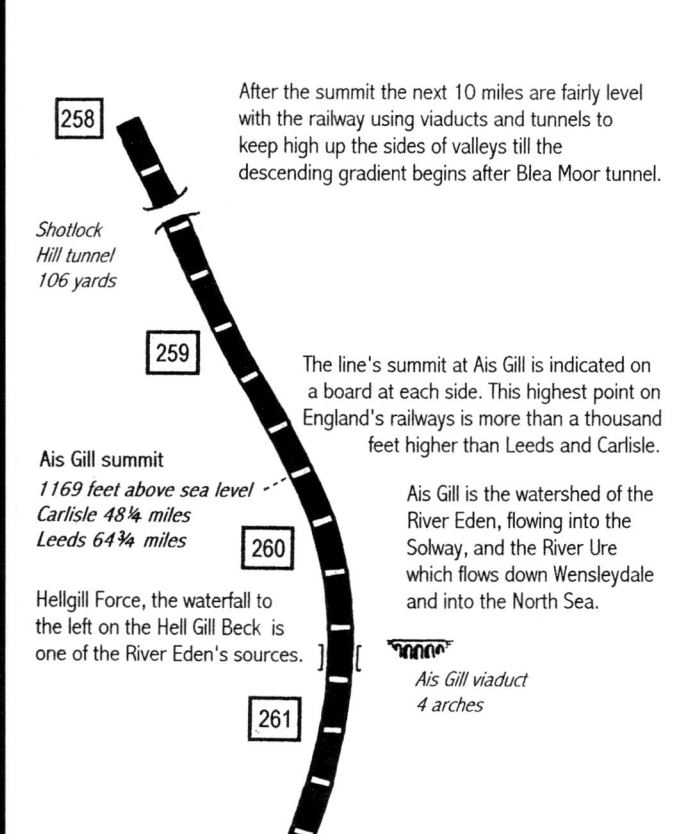

After the summit the next 10 miles are fairly level with the railway using viaducts and tunnels to keep high up the sides of valleys till the descending gradient begins after Blea Moor tunnel.

258

Shotlock Hill tunnel 106 yards

259

The line's summit at Ais Gill is indicated on a board at each side. This highest point on England's railways is more than a thousand feet higher than Leeds and Carlisle.

Ais Gill summit
1169 feet above sea level
Carlisle 48¼ miles
Leeds 64¾ miles

260

Ais Gill is the watershed of the River Eden, flowing into the Solway, and the River Ure which flows down Wensleydale and into the North Sea.

Hellgill Force, the waterfall to the left on the Hell Gill Beck is one of the River Eden's sources.

Ais Gill viaduct 4 arches

261

262

The slopes of Wild Boar Fell rising to 2324 feet are on the right.

263

XII

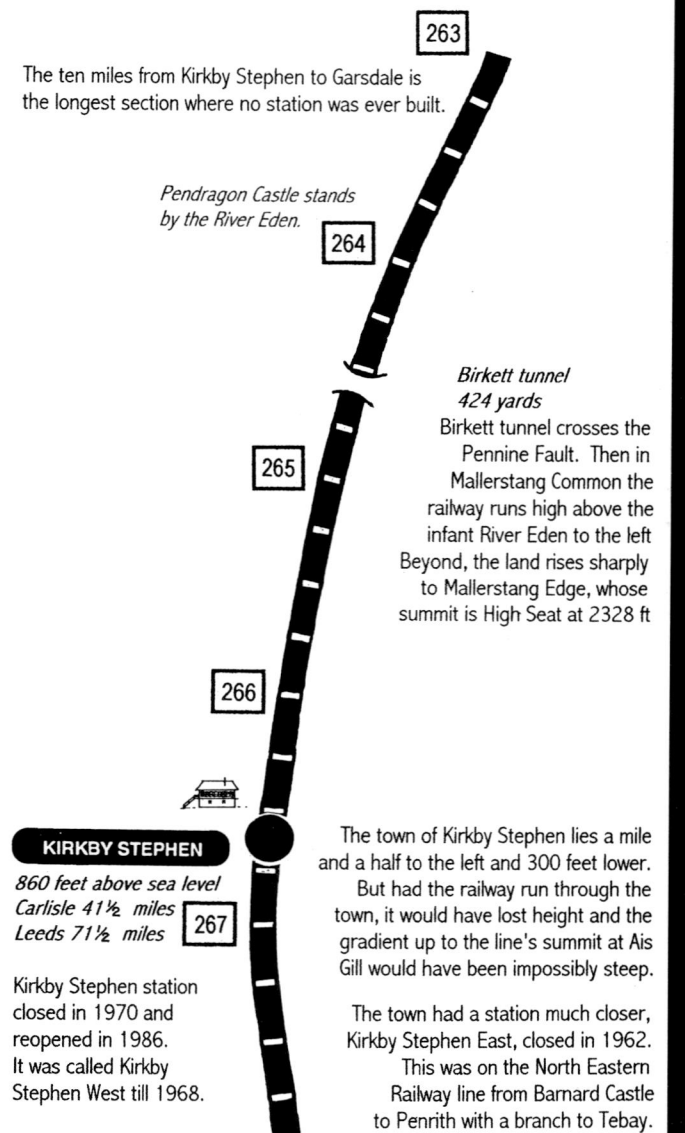

The ten miles from Kirkby Stephen to Garsdale is the longest section where no station was ever built.

263

Pendragon Castle stands by the River Eden.

264

Birkett tunnel
424 yards
Birkett tunnel crosses the Pennine Fault. Then in Mallerstang Common the railway runs high above the infant River Eden to the left Beyond, the land rises sharply to Mallerstang Edge, whose summit is High Seat at 2328 ft

265

266

KIRKBY STEPHEN

860 feet above sea level
Carlisle 41½ miles
Leeds 71½ miles

267

Kirkby Stephen station closed in 1970 and reopened in 1986. It was called Kirkby Stephen West till 1968.

The town of Kirkby Stephen lies a mile and a half to the left and 300 feet lower. But had the railway run through the town, it would have lost height and the gradient up to the line's summit at Ais Gill would have been impossibly steep.

The town had a station much closer, Kirkby Stephen East, closed in 1962. This was on the North Eastern Railway line from Barnard Castle to Penrith with a branch to Tebay.

268

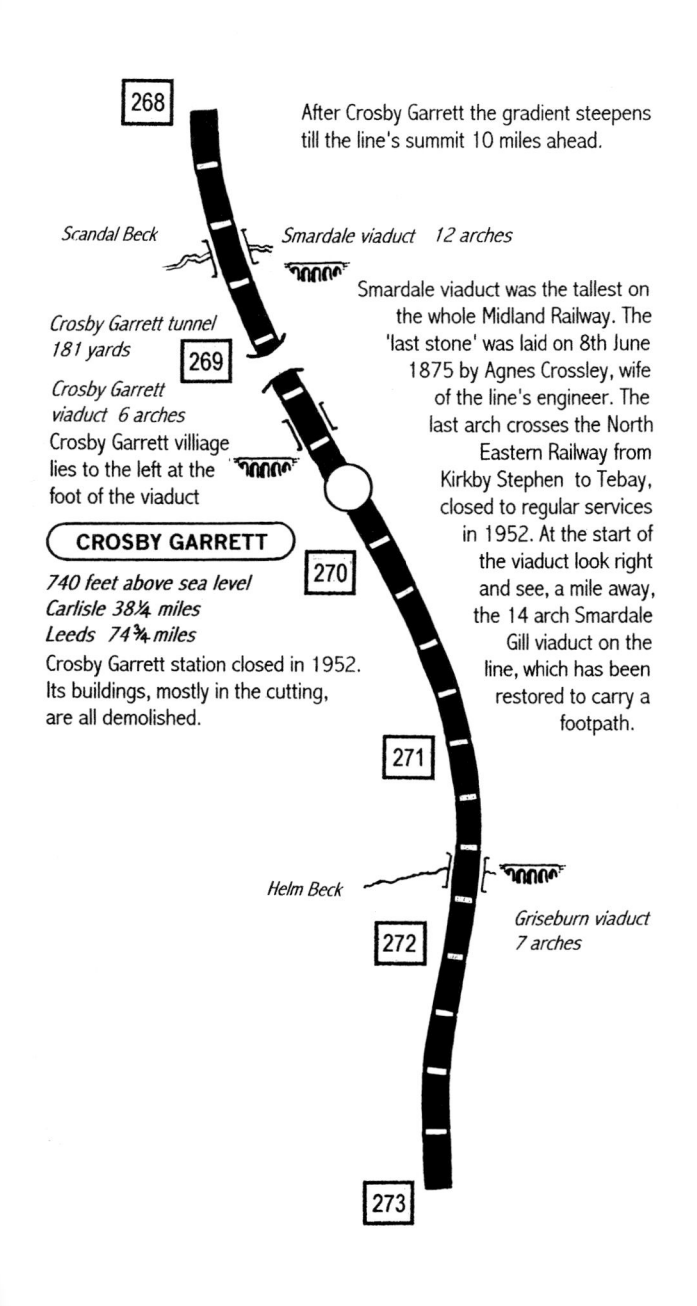

268

After Crosby Garrett the gradient steepens till the line's summit 10 miles ahead.

Scandal Beck

Smardale viaduct   12 arches

*Crosby Garrett tunnel
181 yards*

269

*Crosby Garrett
viaduct 6 arches*
Crosby Garrett villiage
lies to the left at the
foot of the viaduct

Smardale viaduct was the tallest on the whole Midland Railway. The 'last stone' was laid on 8th June 1875 by Agnes Crossley, wife of the line's engineer. The last arch crosses the North Eastern Railway from Kirkby Stephen to Tebay, closed to regular services in 1952. At the start of the viaduct look right and see, a mile away, the 14 arch Smardale Gill viaduct on the line, which has been restored to carry a footpath.

CROSBY GARRETT

*740 feet above sea level
Carlisle 38¼ miles
Leeds 74¾ miles*

Crosby Garrett station closed in 1952. Its buildings, mostly in the cutting, are all demolished.

270

271

Helm Beck

272

*Griseburn viaduct
7 arches*

273

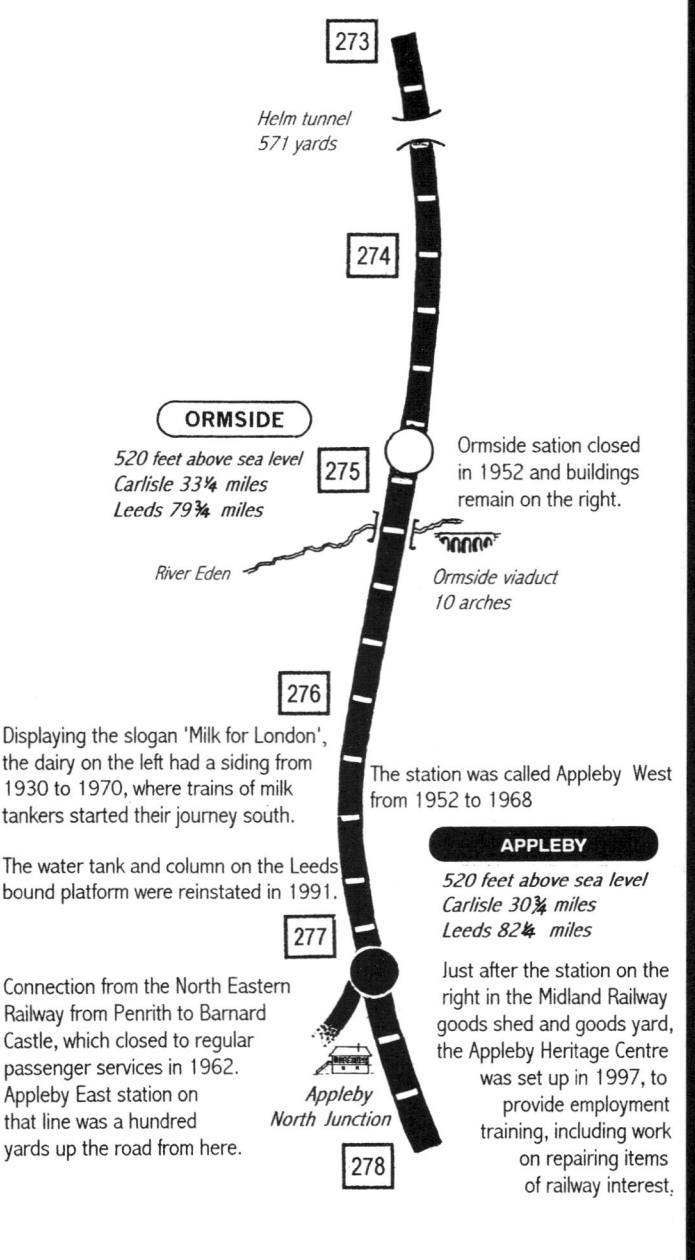

273

*Helm tunnel
571 yards*

274

(ORMSIDE)

*520 feet above sea level
Carlisle 33¼ miles
Leeds 79¾ miles*

275

Ormside sation closed
in 1952 and buildings
remain on the right.

River Eden

*Ormside viaduct
10 arches*

276

Displaying the slogan 'Milk for London',
the dairy on the left had a siding from
1930 to 1970, where trains of milk
tankers started their journey south.

The station was called Appleby West
from 1952 to 1968

The water tank and column on the Leeds
bound platform were reinstated in 1991.

APPLEBY

*520 feet above sea level
Carlisle 30¾ miles
Leeds 82¼ miles*

277

Connection from the North Eastern
Railway from Penrith to Barnard
Castle, which closed to regular
passenger services in 1962.
Appleby East station on
that line was a hundred
yards up the road from here.

*Appleby
North Junction*

Just after the station on the
right in the Midland Railway
goods shed and goods yard,
the Appleby Heritage Centre
was set up in 1997, to
provide employment
training, including work
on repairing items
of railway interest.

278

Carlisle to Leeds →

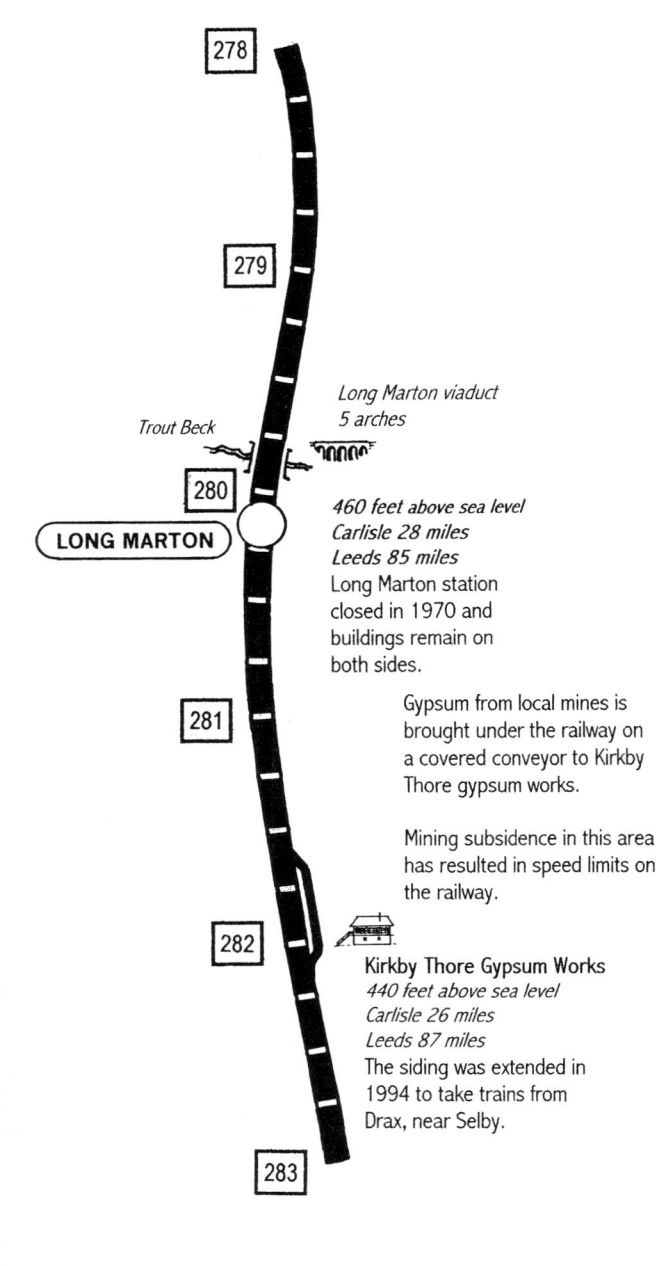

278

279

Long Marton viaduct
5 arches

Trout Beck

280

LONG MARTON

460 feet above sea level
Carlisle 28 miles
Leeds 85 miles
Long Marton station
closed in 1970 and
buildings remain on
both sides.

281

Gypsum from local mines is
brought under the railway on
a covered conveyor to Kirkby
Thore gypsum works.

Mining subsidence in this area
has resulted in speed limits on
the railway.

282

Kirkby Thore Gypsum Works
440 feet above sea level
Carlisle 26 miles
Leeds 87 miles
The siding was extended in
1994 to take trains from
Drax, near Selby.

283

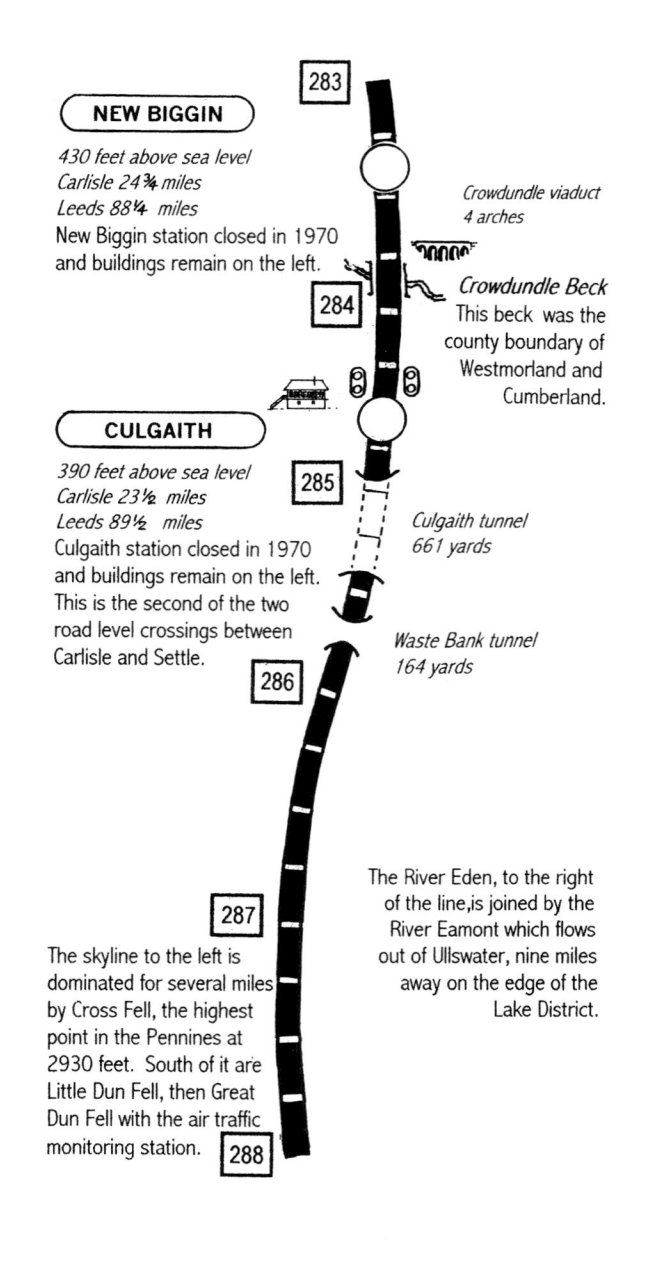

283

NEW BIGGIN

*430 feet above sea level
Carlisle 24¾ miles
Leeds 88¼ miles*
New Biggin station closed in 1970
and buildings remain on the left.

*Crowdundle viaduct
4 arches*

284

Crowdundle Beck
This beck was the
county boundary of
Westmorland and
Cumberland.

CULGAITH

*390 feet above sea level
Carlisle 23½ miles
Leeds 89½ miles*
Culgaith station closed in 1970
and buildings remain on the left.
This is the second of the two
road level crossings between
Carlisle and Settle.

285

*Culgaith tunnel
661 yards*

*Waste Bank tunnel
164 yards*

286

287

The skyline to the left is
dominated for several miles
by Cross Fell, the highest
point in the Pennines at
2930 feet. South of it are
Little Dun Fell, then Great
Dun Fell with the air traffic
monitoring station.

The River Eden, to the right
of the line, is joined by the
River Eamont which flows
out of Ullswater, nine miles
away on the edge of the
Lake District.

288

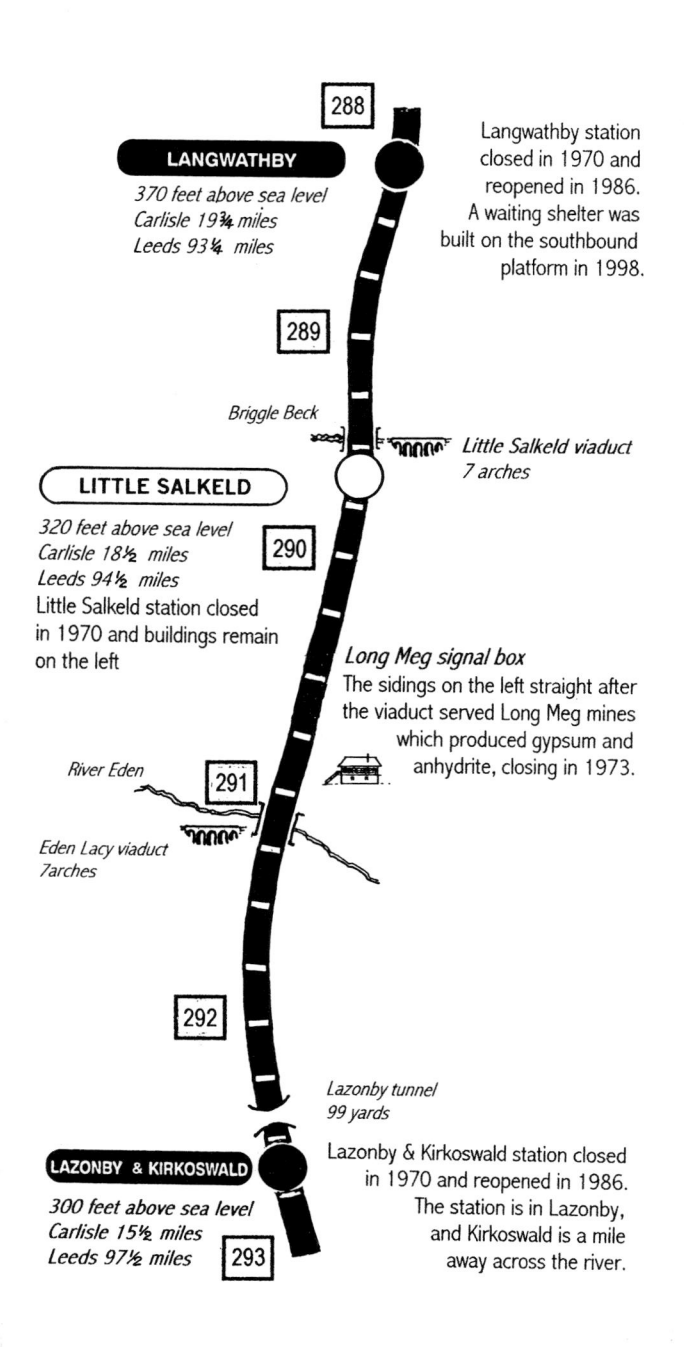

288

LANGWATHBY

370 feet above sea level
Carlisle 19¾ miles
Leeds 93¼ miles

Langwathby station closed in 1970 and reopened in 1986. A waiting shelter was built on the southbound platform in 1998.

289

Briggle Beck

Little Salkeld viaduct 7 arches

LITTLE SALKELD

320 feet above sea level
Carlisle 18½ miles
Leeds 94½ miles
Little Salkeld station closed in 1970 and buildings remain on the left

290

Long Meg signal box
The sidings on the left straight after the viaduct served Long Meg mines which produced gypsum and anhydrite, closing in 1973.

River Eden

291

Eden Lacy viaduct 7 arches

292

Lazonby tunnel 99 yards

LAZONBY & KIRKOSWALD

300 feet above sea level
Carlisle 15½ miles
Leeds 97½ miles

293

Lazonby & Kirkoswald station closed in 1970 and reopened in 1986. The station is in Lazonby, and Kirkoswald is a mile away across the river.

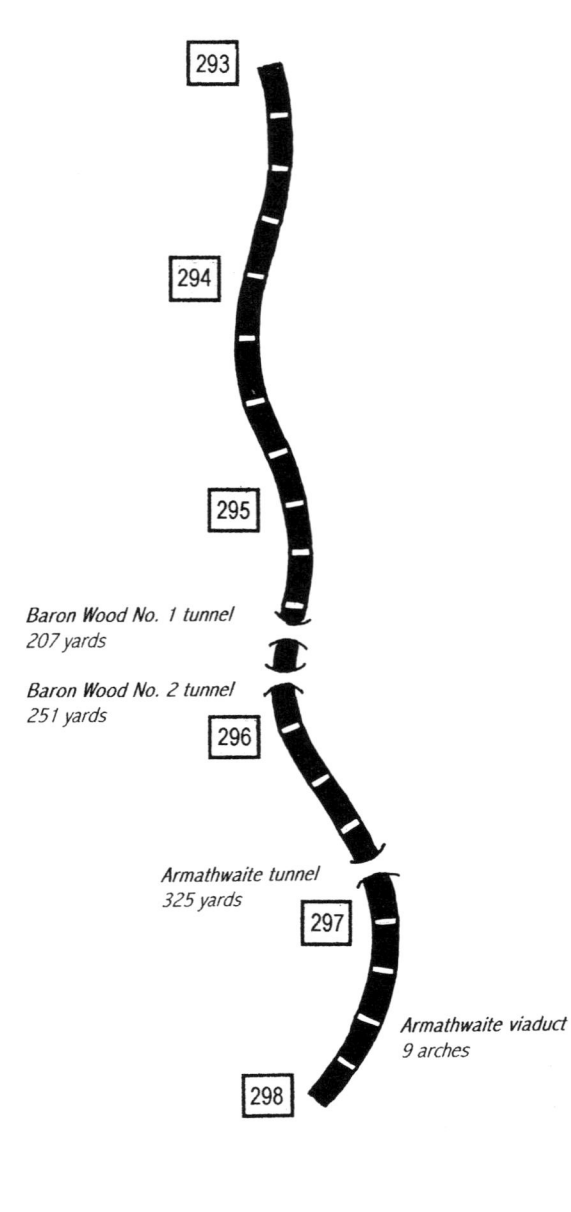

293

294

295

Baron Wood No. 1 tunnel
207 yards

Baron Wood No. 2 tunnel
251 yards

296

Armathwaite tunnel
325 yards

297

Armathwaite viaduct
9 arches

298

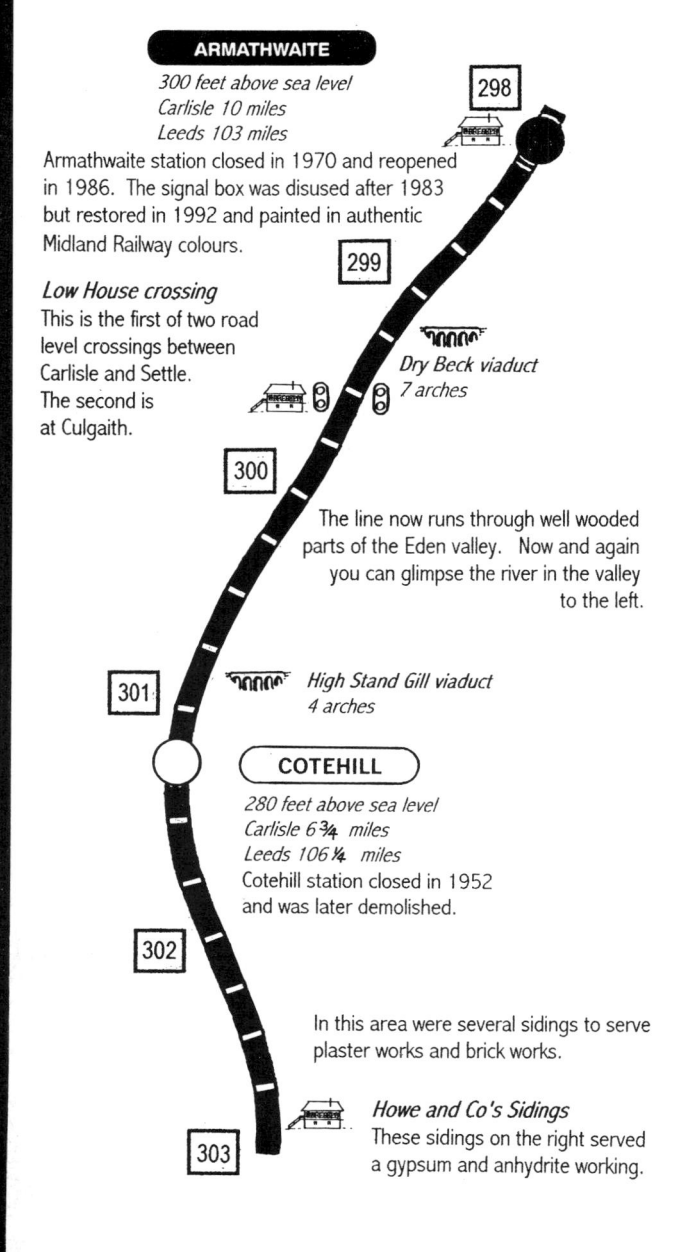

ARMATHWAITE

300 feet above sea level
Carlisle 10 miles
Leeds 103 miles

298

Armathwaite station closed in 1970 and reopened in 1986. The signal box was disused after 1983 but restored in 1992 and painted in authentic Midland Railway colours.

299

Low House crossing
This is the first of two road level crossings between Carlisle and Settle. The second is at Culgaith.

Dry Beck viaduct
7 arches

300

The line now runs through well wooded parts of the Eden valley. Now and again you can glimpse the river in the valley to the left.

301

High Stand Gill viaduct
4 arches

COTEHILL

280 feet above sea level
Carlisle 6¾ miles
Leeds 106¼ miles
Cotehill station closed in 1952 and was later demolished.

302

In this area were several sidings to serve plaster works and brick works.

Howe and Co's Sidings
These sidings on the right served a gypsum and anhydrite working.

303

IV

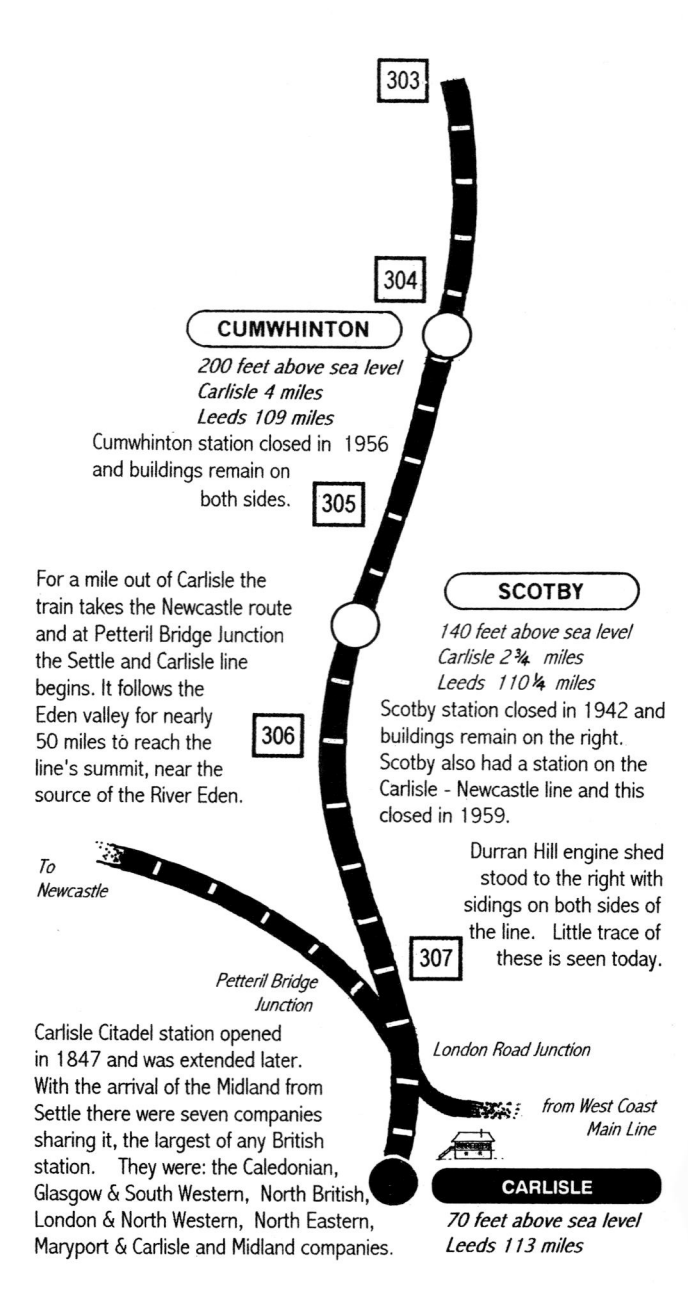

303

304

CUMWHINTON

200 feet above sea level
Carlisle 4 miles
Leeds 109 miles
Cumwhinton station closed in 1956
and buildings remain on
both sides.

305

For a mile out of Carlisle the
train takes the Newcastle route
and at Petteril Bridge Junction
the Settle and Carlisle line
begins. It follows the
Eden valley for nearly
50 miles to reach the
line's summit, near the
source of the River Eden.

SCOTBY

140 feet above sea level
Carlisle 2¾ miles
Leeds 110¼ miles
Scotby station closed in 1942 and
buildings remain on the right.
Scotby also had a station on the
Carlisle - Newcastle line and this
closed in 1959.

306

Durran Hill engine shed
stood to the right with
sidings on both sides of
the line. Little trace of
these is seen today.

307

To
Newcastle

Petteril Bridge
Junction

London Road Junction

Carlisle Citadel station opened
in 1847 and was extended later.
With the arrival of the Midland from
Settle there were seven companies
sharing it, the largest of any British
station. They were: the Caledonian,
Glasgow & South Western, North British,
London & North Western, North Eastern,
Maryport & Carlisle and Midland companies.

from West Coast
Main Line

CARLISLE

70 feet above sea level
Leeds 113 miles

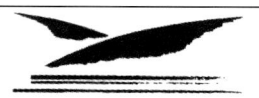
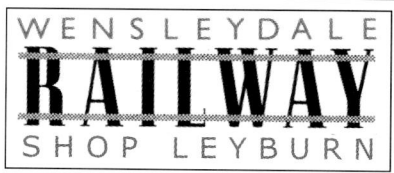

Carlisle to Leeds

For instructions on how to use this guide
please refer to page 21 in the
Leeds to Carlisle section

GREAT NORTHERN